Advent

A spiritual focus for
personal or group use

Hope

A 31-DAY ADVENT GUIDE

JOEL EDWARDS

Contents

Introduction

Some years ago I met with a group of Christian leaders
to talk about how we might raise a message of hope for
people beyond the Church. It led to a lively conversation.
How could we possibly talk about hope in a way that
made sense to people outside the faith? Wasn't the idea of
hope a rather vague Christian doctrine?

But then, a few weeks before writing this Advent study,
I met in the same room to discuss Hope08 – an amazing
nationwide mission that we will talk about later in this
study. Our meeting was a very meaningful time for me as
we looked at the practical ways in which God's hope will
be brought to many thousands of people.

Hope is not an idea; it is God's commitment to the
people He loves.

Every day people languish for hope. Situations confront
us that rob us of the possibility of tomorrow. Memories of
our past behaviour or circumstances, strained relationships
or failed dreams can push us so far into despair that God
becomes a foreigner and hope another language.

It really doesn't matter who you are, when you were
born or where you live: hope is an invaluable commodity.
No one can live without it.

Hope is a very Christian concept. From the earliest
moments of the Fall, God immediately introduced the idea
of hope (Gen. 3:15), and that sense of hope is at the very
heart of Advent – the coming of Jesus. But God's promise
of hope wasn't a start–stop affair. Having made the
promise of hope in the Garden of Eden, God sustained
this promise through the patriarchs, prophets, poetry
and priesthood of the Bible. The whole of Scripture is a
catalogue of God's commitment to bring hope to a world
in waiting.

So in the first week of our studies we will turn to
the book of Isaiah to explore God's provisions of hope
brought to us *from the past*. This section offers a brief

look at what God promised through Isaiah's prophecies about the Messiah long ago. In our second week we will consider how the Bible offers us hope *for our past*. Here we look at some familiar Bible stories to see how God brought hope to people by helping them deal with things they had done or experienced previously. But God's words come to us not only from yesterday; there are also words of hope *for today*. So, in our third week, we will look at John's Gospel and ask how that hope applies to our situation. Week Four will offer us a focus on *hope to live by*, based on a number of character studies from Luke's Advent account. In our final section we'll consider *hope in action* from the book of Acts.

How to Use *Advent Hope*

This Advent guide is flexible enough to be used either for individual or group study. Each day's study will offer a short Bible text and summary. It will also include a brief section entitled 'Doing hope', to help anchor what we have learnt from the Scriptures. We then lead into 'Reflections on hope'. These are not quite the same things as prayer points. The 'Reflections on hope' are there to be used as discussion points, so if you are using this book with a group, do spend some time talking through these before praying about them. If your group meets weekly, you may want to select just a few questions from that week's readings, appropriate to the amount of time you have.

This section will not provide any action points, however. It's easy enough to make up things to do, but I imagine few of us will be able to commit to thirty-one action points in the average month! Instead, at the end of each study there is a 'Creating space to act' section. Take some time to devise personal action points on any issues where you feel the Holy Spirit guiding you to change or act as a result of your reflections and prayer. On some days I have added a prayer which you could pray as written or adapt and personalise.

Advent is a clear reminder that God has acted for our hope, but it also reminds us that hope calls each of us to action in the world. Please don't feel guilty, however, if there's nothing to do at the end of every section! Perhaps giving God thanks is as much as you need to do!

Remember Advent is all about hope.

WEEK ONE
Hope from the Past

A friend once told me that she had come into a small windfall. A relative had left a legacy which included a modest sum of money for her. She hadn't expected it, but it was very welcome!

Legacies are like that. They amount to morsels of blessings that reach out from one generation to another. The past connects with the present and even helps to change the future.

Hope is like that, too. Through the prophets, God sent hope on ahead of us as the people He loves.

In this week's study we will look at Isaiah chapter 9 – a very special Advent passage – and see how God sent hope from the past.

Light to live by

Bible text
Isaiah 9:2–3

> The people walking in darkness
>   have seen a great light;
> on those living in the land of the shadow of death
>   a light has dawned.
> You have enlarged the nation and increased their joy ...

Many years ago I paid a price for getting dressed whilst scrambling around in the dark: I turned up at a young offender's prison to conduct a counselling session wearing two different-coloured shoes! They were very similar styles and indistinguishable in the dark. The boys at the prison were very polite, but I can imagine what they had to say when they got together after I left the scene. Having light to live by is quite an advantage when you have places to go.

God had a very special relationship with His people Israel, but that relationship was never meant to ignore everyone else. And God knew that His own people – the people of the covenant – were in need of light. That was the purpose of the Torah. The Law was given as a lamp to their feet and light for their path (Psa. 119:105). It became evident, however, that Israel needed an even greater light, for as they stumbled through history to live out God's purposes for them as a nation, even the illumination of Moses' Law became dim. Despite the best efforts of the prophets and priests, the people of Israel constantly stumbled in their efforts to be the people of God.

But light was also a provision for the Gentiles. If the people of Israel were the people of covenant then all peoples were the people of promise. And Isaiah more than most prophets was the champion of what the theologian J.I. Packer describes as God's 'cosmic generosity'.

For nothing is darker than not knowing you have hope.

Isaiah's prophecy in this great Advent message is therefore a mark of God's commitment not only to the Jewish people who lived by the shadowy lamp of the Torah, but also to those who lived in outer darkness. That deep darkness was the total unawareness that they were already the objects of God's incessant love. God's intention was clear: nations who stood outside the covenant relationship with Him were to be harmonised into His purposes. Eventually the great wall of separation between Jews and their Gentile neighbours was to be shattered and everyone in every nation and culture would have access to the great Light (John 1:3–9). As a result of this great Light, nations would experience unrestrained joy, like that which farmers sense following a great harvest, or soldiers in dividing the spoils of war.

This story of hope is the recognition that God is everybody's God.

Doing hope

People who walk in darkness are not necessarily bad people. They're lost people.

The hope of Advent is that God has come not to condemn us but to liberate us with the light of His Son Jesus.

If we are to be at our best, getting dressed in the dark is a risky strategy! Isaiah's message is that there is light to live by. That light has come to us in the first instance through the Word of life – the Bible. But, it has come to us supremely through the Living Light – Jesus, who illuminates the world around us from within us so that we can live as God would have us live.

There is no need to stumble about in our private circumstances or public responsibilities. We have light to live by. Those of us who have truly received that light will understand better than most that God has a global agenda of hope for Jews and Gentiles alike. That light leads us to act in such a world.

Reflections on hope

- If Isaiah were alive today, what would he make of his own words as he examined a global Christian faith that has spread across so many nations? What would he be worried about or thankful for?
- More specifically, what would Isaiah pray about if he were considering the relationship between the Jewish people and other nations – especially Arab nations?
- How then can we understand what God is doing now in revealing Himself as a God of hope in Israel, the land of promise? How can we understand what God is doing in the land of promise?

Creating space to act

Imagine being in a room with Isaiah today. He has just read you his word of hope about Jesus as the Light to live by. What might he advise you to do about your own life or the bigger issues in the world on which this Light shines? Pray about this.

2 DEC

Wonderful wisdom

Bible text
Isaiah 9:6

> For to us a child is born,
>   to us a son is given,
>   and the government will be on his shoulders.

As Mary and Joseph swept into the Temple, their anxieties and exhaustion rapidly gave way to incredulity. It had been three days since they last saw Jesus (Luke 2:41–46). From a distance they heard the lilting voice of their twelve-year-old son hovering over the heavier drone of the ancient academic priests. It was only as they came closer and saw the looks on the elders' faces and heard the questions Jesus was asking that they finally stopped worrying and found themselves once again bemused by what they heard and saw.

But they shouldn't have been surprised. As the child grew it must have been very evident that He had a maturity and wisdom beyond His years. At times adults were made uncomfortable by His penetrating questions and insights. He was so young and yet so old.

And that's what Isaiah saw: a child on whom the responsibility of government rested. The child would be known as a wise Counsellor.

In the ancient world with its limited mortality, child kings were not uncommon. However, everyone knew that young monarchs would have a battery of chaperones and counsellors. Isaiah would have known of Uzziah, who became king at the age of sixteen and left the throne fifty-two years later as a leper. He would also have in mind King Solomon, who came to the throne 'young and inexperienced' (1 Chron. 29:1), asking God for wisdom (2 Chron. 1:10). But like Uzziah after him, Solomon started well and ended up in disaster.

So to speak of a king whose wisdom and righteousness would last for infinity was quite a promise. In the Messiah, however, Isaiah foresaw not just a powerful King and mighty God but a Wonderful Counsellor. Jesus as Counsellor ensures a rule with people in mind. He is not just King over the kingdom; He is also Counsellor to the people in the kingdom. His power guarantees His authority as a ruler, but His counsel will show His sovereign care for His subjects.

A king as a counsellor is a precious thing.

Doing hope

There is something quite incredible about the idea that our King is also our Counsellor, for kingship can be a very impersonal and detached bureaucratic response to our humanity. Heaven is not a gigantic switchboard. It gathers around the throne of grace where help is found in times of need (Heb. 4:16).

So we have hope because our King really knows us by name. His wisdom is at our disposal. He counsels us not simply to make us feel better about ourselves but in order that we may be better citizens in the kingdom. No one should assume that having a king as counsellor is meant to be a comfortable experience; the child turned adult King can still be as uncomfortable and bemusing as the young boy in the Temple. It's not just what He knows that makes His counsel wise; it's often the questions He asks of us which makes it so effective.

Wise counsel doesn't necessarily console us but it always guides us, and to sit in this Counsellor's presence can be as demanding as it is empowering. Our Wonderful Counsellor will point us in the right direction in times of uncertainty. He may also point us to the right people when we run out of ideas. His counsel will goad us into right behaviour or say nothing at all, leaving us to apply His grace to our wisdom and experiences. But He is always wonderfully wise whatever path He leads us to take.

Reflections on hope

- Many of us become wiser as we grow older. Our range of experiences and exposures inform our intellect and insight and we develop our understanding of the world and our response to it. However, God's wisdom is another thing altogether. It comes to us for specific situations that need tailor-made insights for effective responses to intractable issues. The question is this: when should we draw on God's counsel as opposed to getting on with things on our own?
- If Christ is to be a Wonderful Counsellor to the nations, how might He be so in today's world? What precisely is our responsibility in bringing this about?
- Western societies which once emulated Christian values and laws are drifting increasingly into post-Christian behaviour. How can the wisdom of Christ be made relevant to our town halls and councils that are more prone to reject the notion of Advent?

Creating space to act

Lord Jesus Christ, I come to You as my Wonderful Counsellor. I bring You the issues of the day most prominent in my mind and ask for Your help and guidance. Amen.

3 DEC

Endless parenting

Bible text
Isaiah 9:6

> And he will be called ...
> Everlasting Father ...

Within a period of ten days in February 2007, five young men were gunned down in London and Moss Side, Manchester. It galvanised the Chief of the Metropolitan Police Service, stirred the Home Secretary into renewed action, pushed the Prime Minister to make a new notice about punishment for gun crimes, resulted in a prayer walk in London and held the news headlines for over a week.

During that period of pain and consternation there were numerous articles and interviews on the subject. In the responses about political and community action there was a recurring theme: most of the young people involved said that the gangs had become their families. Many of us were shocked to learn the extent to which older and more experienced criminals had become surrogate parents for the young men who were desperate for role models.

A biblical response to fatherhood is about a lot more than gender.

There is something quite radical about the idea that God, the Creator of the universe, presents Himself to His creatures as Father. But so He is. Fatherhood begins as a genetic and biological reality. God is Father in the sense that He is the source of our very being (Gen. 1:27; Mal. 2:10; Acts 17:28). There is a sense in which we are all God's children simply because we exist.

But there are three things about the *Messiah* as Father that are really important.

First, fatherhood in the Bible is about spiritual ancestry and historic identity, which is why the Jewish people argued against Jesus that Abraham was their father. However, as Paul explained, Abraham has become the 'father' of everyone who puts their faith in God through Jesus Christ (Rom. 4:11). Second, taking the example of Joseph in Egypt (Gen. 45:8), fatherhood also describes the relationship between a wise counsellor and his leader. Third, fatherhood is about caring. In the Jewish context, fatherhood made no sense without the concept of caring. That was why the story of the Prodigal Son was so powerful as an illustration of a loving father (Luke 15:11–32).

This was what Isaiah was describing in presenting the Messiah's eternal fatherhood. He is our eternal source of wisdom and belonging. Everything comes from Him as the source of life itself (John 1:1–5). And quite clearly our spiritual ancestry comes from Him as our source of salvation (John 1:12–14; Rom. 8:9–17). Also, in the spirit of fatherhood Jesus becomes our Counsellor. Paul discovered this when the 'Spirit of Jesus' stopped him entering Bithynia (Acts 16:7).

To have a father who is living is one thing, but to have a Father who lives forever is quite another.

Doing hope
The idea of God as our Father does not sit easily with everyone. In far too many homes fathers are either missing or malfunctioning. If, like me, you were brought up in a single-parent family, fatherhood can be a real obstacle to faith. My father was a very bad role model. He was physically abusive to my mother and entirely negligent to my siblings and me as his children. Having lived with him for the first eight years of my life, I have very few positive memories of him as a father. When my two children came along I had to re-learn what fatherhood meant!

As Everlasting Father, Jesus, our role model, has come to give us hope.

We really can turn to Him for advice: a help in time of need. His fatherly counsel does not mean always telling us what we want to know. It's more likely to mean telling us what we need to do. The counsel of Christ isn't always accommodating – but this is wise fatherhood.

I recall a conversation some years ago with a teenager who had fallen foul of the law. I asked him what he thought had gone wrong. He said, 'If only my dad had taught me right from wrong I wouldn't be in this mess!' He wasn't just passing the buck – he really was trying to make sense of the mess he was in. Our parenting can make all the difference to those for whom we are spiritually responsible. So how does Christ as a model of parenting work for us?

Reflections on hope

- How much do we recognise ourselves in those for whom we have responsibility? The truth is we are all role models – it's just that some are more positive ones than others. We are often the source of other people's behaviour. Uncles and aunts, mothers and grandfathers – we all bear the responsibility of living lives that bring value and hope to others.
- Hopefully our parenting of those around us will result in positive counselling that helps them work out the difference between right and wrong. How well do we do this in our youth groups or domestic relationships?
- It's always worth remembering that the road to recovery and hope is often a long one. Jesus, our Everlasting Father, has promised to be with us to 'the very end of the age' (Matt. 28:20).

Creating space to act

Perhaps today's focus has raised some difficult issues for you as a parent or spiritual leader. Perhaps it has highlighted your experience as biological or spiritual orphan.

Pray through what you have discovered.

4 DEC

A very big God

Bible text

Isaiah 9:6

> And he will be called
>   Wonderful Counsellor, Mighty God ...

Someone once said that God created man in His own image and then man returned the compliment!

Our image of God is clouded by our finite minds. Eternally ingenious though we are, we lock ourselves into small chambers of reality when compared to God's immense greatness. In understanding God, language and images fail us. But, more than that, they fail God. This is precisely why the Bible warns us against replicating God's image or using His name in vain (Exod. 20:4,7). Jewish people would not speak His name. The God of the Bible is unimaginably immense and our minds stagger to make sense of this greatness (Isa. 40). Not even the expanse of the heavens contains Him (2 Chron. 2:6). But it's not just the immensity of God which challenges us, it's also His pre-eminence. He is before all other gods and is to be compared to no other god (Exod. 20:3).

This Mighty God has no equal and tolerates no co-regent. The intolerant orthodoxy of Judaism meant that throughout their history they often died rather than compromise their monotheistic faith in their Mighty God.

In Isaiah's vision of the future, however, a baby would become God's co-equal as Mighty God – a vision John would later encapsulate in his Gospel (John 1:1–14). When the promised Messiah finally arrived He would be the ultimate stumbling block for the Jewish mind. A man born out of wedlock who ate, slept and broke their laws was incompatible with the Almighty God. It was blasphemy. Only by realising this can we begin to understand how much faith and courage those most closely related to Jesus exercised in believing what the angels said about the child that was born to the virgin woman.

Doing hope

If it is true that people can make God in their image, Christians need to beware. We need to beware particularly at this time of Advent, for ironically there is no other time of the year when we are more likely to forget that the babe is also mighty. In doing so we too easily construct a helpless Jesus whose sovereignty becomes limited to our own notions of who we would prefer Him to be.

In a culture where the concept of 'god' has been relativised to shape the religion of tolerance, Jesus as the Mighty God may be as unpopular for Christians as He was for our Jewish forebears.

Our multi-faith society argues against the uniqueness of any one faith. Amongst the constellation of gods Jesus will often be regarded as a good man, a great teacher or even a revolutionary, but apart from Christians, Jesus is seldom regarded by anyone as the only way to God, and certainly not as the Almighty God.

But if Jesus is to be our Mighty God He must be allowed to be more than a baby: we too must have no other god before Him.

Reflections on hope

- If God is beyond our ability to comprehend Him we will always struggle to make full sense of who He is in our world. Can we make full sense of who He is in our lives?
- Given that it's so hard to capture Jesus as Almighty God with our words, how can our words ever be sufficient to say anything useful about Him? Isn't it best to say nothing, in case we get it wrong every time?
- How are we to defend the idea that Jesus Christ is uniquely different, without being arrogant? The idea of Jesus as a baby helps us to express the humility of our faith, which is far better than the talk of might and power which only leads to competition and arrogance in religion. Isn't this exactly what we should be avoiding at Advent?

Creating space to act

Immortal, invisible, God only wise,
In light inaccessible hid from our eyes,
Most blessed, most glorious, the Ancient of Days,
Almighty, victorious, Thy great name we praise.

(Walter Chalmers Smith)

5 DEC

The promise of peace

Bible text
Isaiah 9:6

And he will be called ...
Prince of Peace.

The last time it happened to me I was out shopping with my wife. At exactly 11am a voice came over the public address system and asked everyone to observe two minutes of silence. A bell pinged and then there was no noise. The sound of peace. Almost nine decades since the Armistice marking the end of the First World War, we still pause at 11am on the 11 November to remember those fallen in battle. And there is something about those two minutes – even for people like me who have never held a gun. It reminds us that peace is more than the absence of war: it is an inward quietness.

Biblical peace – *shalom* – is about a lot more than quiet periods in world history or our personal lives. *Shalom* is a statement of wellbeing. A peaceful person loves God's law and is not easily offended, because their entire mindset is focussed on the God of peace. Peace is not a vacuum created by a non-violent setting; it doesn't appear in the absence of strife or domestic pressures.

The peace that comes from God has a life of its own. Peace is positive quiet. This is because peace has a source: it comes from the Prince of Peace.

Isaiah manages to combine two important thoughts in our verse for today. Firstly, that this hope of peace is sustained by a Person with the authority to give peace. This great Son will be authorised to dispatch peace because He is peace personified. The Messiah, Isaiah says, will be the principal source of peace. Second, the fact that He is Prince makes Him subject to the King. He is still the Son given to us. The Prince of Peace does not usurp the God of peace (Phil. 4:9; 1 Thess. 5:23; Heb. 13:20).

So Advent was filled with the hope of Jesus' peace (Luke 2:14). So powerful and present is His peace that even the sea gives way to it (Mark 4:39). His peace was to be a distinguishing mark of His personal relationship with those who followed Him. 'My peace I leave with you,' He told them (John 14:27).

And finally, Jesus brought God's peace to us by His incredible sacrifice on the cross (Col. 1:20).

Doing hope

We should never forget that the peace of God comes to us in the forgiveness of our sin. Peace with God is the story of sins forgiven. To be justified by Christ's death is to be at peace with God (Rom. 5:1).

And there is no greater peace. This peace is the first and greatest hope of humankind. It's peace on the inside.

It is a big mistake to assume that peace happens outside of us and inside our circumstances. If we know the Prince of Peace we need not wait for things around us to change in order to experience the power of peace. If we know the Prince we may know His peace – whatever is happening around us. Peace penetrates our problems, and in the very centre of our storms we find the space to be still and hopeful.

But it's more than that. Peace receivers are also called to be peacemakers (Matt. 5:9). Because they serve the Prince of Peace, peacemakers are courageous people. It's easy enough to assume that peaceful people prefer to give conflicts a wide birth; to keep their heads down and mind their own business. In fact it's only too easy to judge the quality of our peace by our ability to smell trouble a mile off and avoid it at all costs! But by definition, peacemakers are usually discovered in war zones.

Those who share the life of the Prince of Peace will get punched precisely because they make peace their business!

Reflections on hope

- It's so much easier to focus on our problems than our source of peace. Sometimes this is because we don't have a very clear idea of precisely what it is that causes our lack of peace. We may need to count our problems – to name them one by one in order to know what we need to let go of.
- If you know the absence of tensions it might be that you are walking in a 'quiet place'. Or it could simply be that you have become very good at avoiding trouble. However, if you are in the absence of interpersonal pressures and living in the place of sheer bliss, it could just mean you're not a very good peacemaker. Which might it be?

Creating space to act

If you were to write a job description for a Prince of Peace, would you be a miniature version?

6 DEC

Just governance

Bible text
Isaiah 9:7

> He will reign on David's throne
>   and over his kingdom,
>   establishing and upholding it
>   with justice and righteousness
>   from that time on and for ever.

Politics is in real trouble. There's nothing wrong with politics itself; the problem is our politicians. And you know it's true when politicians themselves tell us. Frankly, there is a sense of hopelessness that covers politics today. There's little difference between governments in our Western democracies and dictators. All governments have become associated with 'spin' or corruption, power games or outright deceit.

Despite the vast majority of political leaders who work tirelessly and sacrificially in their commitment to the people they serve, politics has become the business of hollow practices and low expectations.

In time, however, all governments come and go. Even great dynasties dissipate under the strain of government. Humanity is now old enough to know that all government and governance is limited by the imperfections of our fallen leaders and the harsh and unforgiving attitudes of the general public. Even the great Christian aspirations of Calvin's Geneva, Cromwell's England and the Pilgrim Fathers' America failed the test.

So the idea of a just and righteous kingdom that has no end is bound to hold some attraction for us. Isaiah is keen to have us realise that God has not abandoned the idea of good and lasting governance. In God's plans it is still scheduled to happen.

This kingdom would flow, not from Saul, the first king of Israel, but from David. Saul was the people's king who failed to obey God and was never promised the kingdom in perpetuity (1 Sam. 13:13–14).

It was to David that this promise of an everlasting kingdom was made (2 Sam. 7:11–16). When Jesus came His kingdom embraced the Davidic heritage and refilled it with hope for the future. In this kingdom everything that is needed for human flourishing is included: peace, sustainability, justice and righteousness. Nothing is missing.

Isaiah's vision is not a picture of the Brave New World of Utopia. The vision is presented to us for two reasons. First, to tell us that God is committed to this ultimate kind of governance; a world in which His kingdom eventually comes on earth and His will is done here as in heaven. This is the hope of our future. Second, Isaiah opens us up to a model of good governance with the idea that we should emulate these principles in our political systems in the here and now. Just and righteous government is not solely the idea of political philosophy; it's also the heartbeat of our public witness.

Doing hope

It's far too easy for us to blame our leaders for the empty hope in our political systems, but we should remember that in a democracy we don't just get the politicians we deserve, we get the public figures we create. In a sense we have a tremendous responsibility to constantly hold up to our politicians a vision of a hope-filled society which will never be perfect but can always be better than it is at present.

We can be hope-bringers to the injustices and unrighteousness in our world. Some years ago I was one of three Christian leaders who provided evidence at one of the high-profile enquiries surrounding the brutal racist murder of a young black man, Stephen Lawrence. At the end of the session we were approached by the senior police officer responsible for the enquiry. What he said was very revealing. He had been to a large number of enquiries by this time but our submission, he said, though as hard-hitting as any other he had received, had somehow left him with a sense of hope. This meant that two of our number became more formally involved in public responsibilities with the police service.

God is likely to call increasing numbers of us to become active citizens bringing light and hope to the world of politics. This really is a very good time to have more followers of the Prince of Peace engaged in the battle for peace. Many of us will be able to bring hope by our financial support to those who work with the poor or those who are the poor. It may mean a gap year in another country or contributing some time to support organisations or individuals in a voluntary capacity.

Reflections on hope

- There are many Christians who give the impression that Christian hope is all about political activism or social kindness. Others are very sceptical about any involvement in actions which challenge prejudice or injustice of any kind. 'Let's pray about it and leave it to God!' they say. Does either response reflect the spirit of Isaiah?
- The good news is that we are now in a world where politicians of all kinds have come to welcome Christian and faith involvement in public life.
- Many Christians already work in politics. What can we do to support them in this tough task of creating just governance?

Creating space to act

Maybe a good space to reflect on some of these ideas is outside your town hall, civic centre or even your parliament. If you're likely to pass a government building in the near future, book yourself some thinking space.

7 DEC

A real throne

Bible text
Isaiah 9:7

> He will reign on David's throne
>   and over his kingdom,
> establishing and upholding it
>   with justice and righteousness ...

Faith is often mistaken for fiction, and it's quite understandable. Everything about Advent is amazing. Angels and virgins; wise men and shepherds seeing visions; genocide and celebrations all make up a picture of a very fanciful story. It may well be that a part of the strength of the Christmas message is its appeal to children. For generations they have had their imaginations fired by tales which fit perfectly into the genre of the Hollywood stories over the Christmas period. Advent and Christmas becomes just another composition in the list of fabricated stories that help us fill the time.

However, King David was no myth. Isaiah's reference to David's throne is a critical inclusion in a catalogue of descriptions about the Messiah which anchor the passage in historic reality. The Messiah is not a Disney invention; He was a Man who could trace His genealogy back to the most famous and celebrated king Israel has ever had.

It was this very fact that the Gospel writers drew on as they sought to convince their readers of the historic truth of the story about the Messiah, Jesus, many years later (Matt. 1:1,6; Luke 2:4).

The coming King was, therefore, no mere figment of the prophet's imagination. Isaiah saw this as a clear testimony of Jesus' claim to rule. The same Wonderful Counsellor and Mighty God was the distant Son of David, Israel's most renowned king.

Doing hope

As we enter Advent we do more than acknowledge an old ritual with no meaning. Christ the Messiah was as real as His forefather David.

This is an important point to realise as every Advent season is associated with headlines attempting to discredit the historic claims about Jesus. This is not novel. For the past 2,000 years this story has endured such claims. The revelation of Jesus Christ really can be trusted not merely as good story with a strong moral message but as a reliable fact of human history.

Our faith stands on the bedrock of tried and tested accounts of God's intervention in the real world. David's throne is a brief reminder that the God who stands beyond history also works within time and space. Little wonder that of the sixty-six books in the Bible thirteen of them are historical documents – about one-fifth. The book of Acts records more historic places and named civic leaders than miracles.

But it's also a reminder that God is interested in real people.

David was a real king but he was also a real man. He was flawed and fallen, but was a king after God's own heart who also *won* the heart of God and emerged from his own personal disasters to help us in our worship of the living God.

We enter Advent on safe grounds.

Reflections on hope

- David's throne remains very central to Jews and Christians alike: isn't this confusing? If Jesus sits on David's throne aren't we therefore under the Old Testament Law instead of God's grace?
- If God has really acted in history, why is it that so many people still doubt that Jesus is who He says He is?
- In the 1970s people talked a lot more about 'evidence' that Jesus existed. Why is it that there is much less discussion about this today? Is it that more people believe He existed or that it doesn't matter to them anymore?

Creating space to act

As the first Christian historian, Luke was very keen to include details in his Gospel account. Why not read slowly through Luke 2:1–4 and ask what was he trying to accomplish in this brief but detailed passage.

WEEK TWO
Hope for the Past

All of us have a story to tell; it's a story of failure or failings. My story includes incidents where my behaviour or circumstances were so painful that I would prefer not to go back there in a year, never mind a *month*, of Sundays.

For many of us, these memories haunt our sleep or conversations and buzz words trigger vivid action-replays in our minds. Our past can so intimidate us that we fail to grasp the present with confidence. It can tie us down and hold us back from our future potential. When our past actions continue to condemn us in the present, hope for the future can be hard to contemplate.

The hope of Advent is the message of retrospective hope. God deals with our past in such a way that it need not steal our hope for the future.

As an African proverb puts it: 'Yesterday is another country: I no longer live there.'

Back to the beginning

Bible text
Exodus 4:19

> Now the LORD had said to Moses in Midian, 'Go back to Egypt,
> for all the men who wanted to kill you are dead.' So Moses
> took his wife and sons, put them on a donkey and started back
> to Egypt.

Egypt was a place of mixed memories for Moses. A genetic Hebrew
and cultural Egyptian, his own identity was called into question when
he saw a Hebrew slave brutalised by an Egyptian slave-driver. Moses
killed the Egyptian only to discover that he had been seen (Exod.
2:11–14). Fleeing Egypt was a desperate move to escape a desperate
and confusing situation. It was bad enough that he had killed in order
to defend his own people, but then the very people he defended
refused to regard him as a saviour. Was his response to the slave-
driver some kind of premonition about his future role as deliverer or
just the impulse of a very angry young man (see Acts 7:25)? Whatever
it was, it seemed the very people he wanted to protect were not
about to cover his back, so there was nowhere else to go.

For forty years Moses ran away from his past until God called out
to him from a burning bush that refused to burn up (Exod. 3:1–4)!
His commission was to return to Egypt. But returning to Egypt would
have been the last thing on Moses' mind – which was why he made
so many excuses (Exod. 4:5–14). Yet it was precisely the place he
feared that became the place of mission and purpose for him. Moses
had left in secret, now he must return to take centre stage. He had
left a murderer, now he was to return as a deliverer. He had left

as an Egyptian prince but now he was to return, staff in hand, as a Hebrew freedom fighter.

Moses was returning to the same place but he was now returning with his mind in a very different place.

Doing hope

Many years ago I pastored a young woman who had recently become a Christian and was terrified of her ex-boyfriend. He had a terrible habit of showing up and dominating her home. He would empty her fridge and generally abuse her generosity and her home – without thinking to support either her or her children. He was a part of her past which really crippled her hope for the future.

When I asked why she allowed him to exert so much power over her, she said that she was afraid of him. Like so many people in her position, she failed to recognise just how afraid she already was! So we learnt an exercise. I suggested that any time her ex-boyfriend came to the home she should walk behind him and talk to him in her head. She was to tell him that he was now a part of her past, that he no longer had any kind of power over her and that this was her home and her life and these were her children; he would have no power over her future.

A few weeks later she plucked up the courage to tell him! She retrieved her house keys and he ceased to exploit her, only visiting on her terms.

For many people the past represents a very strange place of confused identities and unresolved questions. Escape comes with a better standard of living, a new location or even a name change. Many of us are petrified to return to the place or experience from which we fled.

But so often God calls us to do precisely that: like the disciples heading back to Jerusalem for Pentecost, God sends us back to encounter the very places of embarrassment, shame or failure. He does this not to rub our noses in it, but to reassure us that our past need not stifle our hope for the future.

Advent offers us hope for our past failures.

Reflections on hope

- Many people are only too aware of how much their past stands before them in the present. Like someone with a sinister pain, they prefer to ignore their past for as long as possible – only to find that the pain gets worse. Sometimes God uses burning bushes to get people to face their fears about the past. He may even use Bible notes ...
- But it's also true that others have so carefully filed away their past that it only emerges in unconscious reactions to things in the present. How can they come to realise this? What happens if other people notice this a lot more easily than they do?
- If God had to threaten Moses before he had a change of mind, does He have to shock us all into co-operating before we revisit the things we would rather leave behind?

Creating space to act

Father God, I want to deal with my past failures. Show me what I need to learn from them and help me to move on, knowing that they need hinder me no more. Amen.

9 DEC

Wiping the slate clean

Bible text
Isaiah 1:18

> 'Come now, let us reason together,' says the LORD. 'Though your sins are like scarlet, they shall be as white as snow; though they are red as crimson, they shall be like wool.'

Debt is another way that the past hangs over our heads.

When a debt is lifted it means that the weight of our past has been adjusted in favour of our future. Anyone who has had a fine or debt cancelled or a driving ban lifted knows something of what Isaiah was talking about.

Although Isaiah has more to say to us about God's hope through the Messiah than any other prophet, there are few chapters in the Bible which start off with such condemnation. Isaiah addresses a nation bowed down with a burden of guilt, whose rebellion makes them prime targets for judgment. So serious is their debt that God has no place for their sacrifices (v.11) or festivals or prayers (vv.14–16). Their religious hyper-activity does not impress Him at all. What He is looking for is justice for the marginalised (v.17) – and a robust conversation (v.18)!

The accumulation of past sins lingering around the Temple worship was the burden that blocked the Jews' hopes and their future. And it was this lingering burden of debt that God wanted to talk to them about so urgently. 'Come now,' He said.

And it didn't matter how desperate their past had been – there was forgiveness. Deep-red sins could be dealt with. Biblical sin was red – not black; for nothing was as ugly as the colour of wasted and sacrilegious blood. The contrast between the red-dye guilt of debt and the innocence of the driven snow is reconciled by forgiveness.

Clearly there was a lot to talk about. This was to be a rigorous conversation of a lifetime, not an easy chat between chums. The debt was serious and the conversation had to be also. But it would be life-changing, for repentance would bring a better future (vv.19–20).

If Advent is about nothing else it is about the hope of forgiveness. You must 'give him the name Jesus', the angel told Mary, 'because he will save his people from their sins' (Matt. 1:21). Hope begins when the past has been dealt with.

Doing hope

One of the most graphic descriptions of forgiveness I have ever heard came from a young man who had a history of depression. 'It's like an electrical circuit,' he said. 'When you pray to God and ask for forgiveness it's like flicking the switch on the wall. The circuit is completed and the light comes on.'

It's not a perfect analogy but you get the point. There's something about the act of saying 'sorry' to another person which has a way of dealing with the past and cancelling the social and relational debt. For many people with a negative relationship hanging over their heads, all they want is an apology; recognition that the past has been smeared and the stains are still painful to everyone concerned. 'Sorry' locks off the past and brings hope for the future.

There is little prospect of real or lasting hope when there are oppressive spiritual debts. Future hope is only secured when our past has been wiped clean. 'Peace with God' only really comes when we have dealt with our lingering debt of rebellion (Rom. 5:1). To build a future without past forgiveness is to build second-best.

We've got to have the conversation.

For all of us, wiping the slate has to take into account two sets of relationships. First, our relationship with God, who is always ready and waiting to talk about liberating us from the sins of the past. Second, our relationships with those with whom we live or work; our fellow slate-cleaners! Peace with God often depends on how we get along with one another.

Reflections on hope

- Many people have things from the past they will never ever forgive. Does God behave in this way or does He really forgive everything we have done if we say 'sorry'?
- Some people tend to say 'sorry' to God quite often. Why is this, do you think? Surely if we say sorry for something once that's good enough, or should we keep reminding God that we really are sorry? Why do we say 'sorry' every week in our church services? Surely fixation with our past sins is very unhealthy. What do you think?
- What should we do if we say 'sorry' to others but they don't want to listen? Do we need to keep apologising? How often do we need to ask for forgiveness in order to be better people? If our friends or relations refuse to let us off, does that mean we are always guilty or does the guilt go away?
- What should we do about people who feel guilty because they can't forgive others? Is Advent and the message of hope a total waste of time for them?

Creating space to act

Lord Jesus, I am truly sorry for the wrong things I have done. Please reach into my past and wipe the slate clean once and for all, and give me hope for the future. Then, in understanding what it means to be forgiven, help me to show forgiveness to others. Amen.

10 DEC

Failure and favour

Bible text
Matthew 1:6

> David was the father of Solomon, whose mother had been
> Uriah's wife ...

It has to be one of the most dramatic cases of sin recorded in the
Bible. It was bad enough that David stayed home in the season
when kings went out to war. And it was inappropriate for him to be
peeking at Bathsheba while she was taking a bath. But to follow that
with adultery, deception, conspiracy to murder and the murder of a
loyal subject is the most shocking example of serial misdemeanours
committed by any one individual in the Bible (2 Sam. 11:1–27).

When David was brought back to his senses by Nathan the prophet,
he was devastated by the depth of his own sin (2 Sam. 12). Not only
was he mortified by his wrongdoing, it seemed that his behaviour
continued to haunt him through his own domestic upheavals, a
national rebellion and even public humiliation at the hands of an
obscure Benjamite (2 Sam. 13–16). Apart from his serious mistake in
numbering the troops (2 Sam. 24) this was the lowest ebb in David's
entire reign as king.

David couldn't have imagined how his life would have been
recorded many years later. Matthew's record demonstrates something
else: people after God's own heart can experience redemption
– even in their most abject failings. David's serious mistakes were the
very foundations on which God was able to work in establishing His
promise to David. It was Solomon, the son of a serious mistake, who
was to carry the promise – not Absalom, the pin-up prince.

God can redeem our worst disasters. Gibeah of Benjamin became
a focus of such moral depravity that the entire nation of Israel rose
up to punish the city (Judg. 19–20), but it was this same town from
which the first king of Israel was chosen. In God's purposes the
'wicked men of Gibeah' (Judg. 20:13) became 'the Gibeah of God'
(1 Sam. 10:5).

The story of Advent is that God was about to deal with the stockpile of Israel's sins in the final work of Jesus the Messiah. Hope for the Jewish people and the world was the recognition that God was about to reach into their past and make better sense of all their failures and failings by fulfilling His promise to show them His favour. The hope of Advent in this regard is that God was not about to discard the nation because of their failings, but to favour them because of His promise to them.

The sorrow of Advent is that apart from a small number, the Jewish people failed to grasp this truth and missed the moment they had long waited for (John 1:10–18).

Doing hope

In varying degrees, all of us have situations in our past or present that make us feel entirely useless to God. Failings and failures which in our own eyes – and often in the eyes of those we have failed – seem irredeemable. We have told ourselves that God can only discard our failures and use our virtues. But that is not true.

God's sovereignty means that He is able to recycle the very disasters He finds repulsive in our past or present lives.

What really matters is that we understand two things. First, that repentance is very powerful. God takes our sins very seriously indeed – but He pays even more attention to our sorrow. The second thing is as important: our relentless commitment to God's purpose in our lives will always influence His attitudes to our failure and our attitudes to ourselves. When God applies His grace to our weakness He does so in order to transform us, not patch us up. And sometimes our painful pasts become present tools in His hands.

The story is told of a village in which an old sculptor frequently visited the local scrapyard. As people went into the scrapyard to throw away their old or battered items, they might see the sculptor emerging with the very pieces they had stockpiled for the furnace. One day there was a great commotion in the middle of the village for there stood a life-sized model of a local hero who had never been commemorated. It stood gleaming in the afternoon sun with the old man polishing and applying the finishing touches to the metallic image. Everyone recognised that the new monument was made from their discarded items.

Out of the ashes of our worst mistakes God relentlessly builds His purpose. Even if you have failed, a failing doth not a failure make!

Reflections on hope

- What would David say if he were reading the Advent lesson from Matthew 1:6? Would he be pleased, or even more embarrassed than he was at the time?
- If God really does have the ability to fix our past faults and failures, doesn't this mean that we can do whatever we like? How do we review our past failings without becoming smug about them?
- Does God always receive the glory from our failures or are there some things we will never ever recover from? What happens if, as in David's case, we never live to see how God uses our past mistakes for the benefit of others?

Creating space to act

Forget about your failures for a moment – past or present! Do you know someone who is going through a time of abject failure now, and for whom the sense of doom is very real?

What can you do for them this Advent?

11 DEC

Everything counts

Bible text

Genesis 45:7–8

> But God sent me ahead of you to preserve for you a remnant on earth and to save your lives by a great deliverance. So then, it was not you who sent me here, but God. He made me father to Pharaoh ...

At what point did Joseph know this? It was unlikely that the thought had dawned on him when he first shared his ambitious dreams with his brothers and parents in the family home (Gen. 37:5–9). It also seems very unlikely that he thought about being any kind of saviour when he found himself at the bottom of a disused well or later in prison in Egypt. And how much was he aware of where his life was going when he became the head of Potiphar's household (39:1–7)? How would he have felt when his master's wife cruelly lied about him and placed him in serious danger (39:13–20)? Would he have felt a sense of destiny when he received those flashes of insight when interpreting other people's dreams (40–41)? Was it at the point when the king of Egypt elevated him to the role of Prime Minister (41:41)?

In the presence of his trembling brothers Joseph made an amazing statement: God meant it all for good. All that had happened between them had been an elaborate design on God's part. Joseph hadn't just turned up in Egypt: he was sent. His arrival was not an evolution of random circumstances but an outcome of God's intentions. And that meant that everything was somehow a part of that plan.

As we saw in our previous study, God is able to use our failures and turn them to His advantage. Joseph came to realise that God used all his experiences to make sense of where He always meant him to be.

Imagine how important this was for Joseph's brothers. All at once their guilt was tempered by the realisation that even their jealous cruelty had been put to good use and they were unwitting accomplices in God's plans to save the world from starvation. What began as a family squabble and petty jealousy between siblings turned out to be a world event.

Hope for the world started with Joseph's slavery.

Joseph's realisation was also important for him because it enabled and empowered him to take the rough with the smooth and put the good and the bad in his past in their proper perspective. Hope for the past meant that Joseph could celebrate with the people who had betrayed him and sold him into slavery.

Doing hope

I can vouch for Joseph's story.

When I left Jamaica at the age of eight it was very hard to imagine that this was part of God's plan. Two years earlier my mother fled our home because of my father's cruelty to her. It was quite an ordeal to wake up one morning when I was little more than six years old and learn that my mother had quietly left for Britain the day before. And it was mysterious and lonely to leave all my friends and the things that were familiar to me to board a plane for an eternal ride to England.

Subsequently, the isolation of being only one of two Christians in a school of 1,200 boys and the huge but eventful culture shocks of Bible college and fourteen years as a probation officer amounted to one thing: I was always in the process of being called. If I tell anyone today that I have a feeling of being sent, it only makes sense in the light of all of those strange as well as enjoyable experiences.

Few of us will end up saving entire nations from starvation, but all of us have been sent to do something. The ups and downs in our lives that feel like immoveable boulders or incredible opportunities often turn out to be important stepping stones to the main platforms of God's purposes for our lives.

This realisation that our past makes up the path to a future in which God is still at work should enable us to let the bad things go as we recognise that both good and bad form the cobblestones to our pathway. Inevitably, people will have hurt or abused us along the way, but we should learn to include them in the celebrations.

Hope for our past reassures us this Advent that God uses all the circumstances in our lives to get us to where He is sending us.

Reflections on hope
- What might have happened had Joseph become bitter along the way? He had enough reasons to become so!
- What kept him going, through imprisonment, slander and slavery? Was it his belief that his dreams meant he still had something to work towards?
- How easy was it for Joseph to really let go of the bad stuff done to him by his brothers in order to celebrate the good? Can we really celebrate what God is doing in our lives if we fail to forgive others for the bad they have done to us?

Creating space to act
Lord, help me to trust that everything that happens in my life can be

used for Your glory. Help me to let go of past hurts and celebrate
Your goodness. Amen.

12 DEC

More than a winner

Bible text
Romans 8:36–37

> As it is written: 'For your sake we face death all day long; we
> are considered as sheep to be slaughtered.' No, in all these
> things we are more than conquerors through him who loved us.

Nobody wants to be on the losing side in a competition. I still have
very vivid memories of school days when the five-a-side team was
being picked for the playground match. The two captains would
stand facing the candidates, who stood in a straight line. Each
captain would take it in turns to choose someone for his team until
there was no one left. If you were one of the last two or three to be
picked, make no mistake about it, it was a statement of your ability
– or inability – to play the game! Captains always went for the best
because they wanted to win.

This leads us to consider something very puzzling about the
Christian faith. Most of us think that God has chosen His winning
team from the bottom of the pile!

Our text for today, which stands directly at the heart of Paul's
teaching about the sustainable nature of our faith, is one of my
very favourite passages that reassures and encourages our faith in
God. Everything works out for good, Paul says (Rom. 8:28). In fact,
those who are called and included in God's programme of salvation
turn out to be 'more than conquerors' because of Christ's love and
commitment to us.

We all know that a conqueror is someone who fights and wins.
What more could you ask for? But, how on earth can you be 'more
than' a winner? This baffled me throughout my teenage years until

I listened to a diminutive Methodist lay preacher. 'A conqueror is someone who fights and wins,' she said. 'But a "more than a conqueror" is someone who fights and cannot lose!'

Paul understood how incredible this claim was, but was quite resolute about it: there really isn't anything that can pull us away from God's love for us. Not even death or life, angels or demons can do it (Rom. 8:38–39). None of the extremes in life have the ability to take us away from God. Neither can things present or things in the future. And that's quite important, for God's ability to save really is timeless.

When the future arrives the present will have become the past. Hope is retrospective. There is nothing in our history that can put a wedge between us and God's love for us today. Christians are more than winners because what Jesus the Messiah has done for us encompasses everything in every age.

Doing hope

Barry Grantham was a very successful man. He had a great family and a fabulous home. He was a successful entrepreneur with a thriving business in the retail industry. He was loved and admired and had everything to live for.

However, no one knew just how much his past tormented him. There seemed to be something to do with his father that he never felt relaxed enough to explore. Granddad was the one subject the kids approached with caution. It was the one thing in the past that made Barry feel like a loser in the present.

There are many people like Barry. Whenever they look over their shoulder there is an ugly giant standing in the shadows to remind them of something. It's the one thing they cannot speak of. It has become a no-go area they dare not explore, and in their worst moments it leaps forward in time to make them feel like losers. No one else can understand just why it is that they are so floored and intimidated by it, for in all other respects they have everything going for them. Or, at the very least, life looks quite good.

Jesus is only our Saviour if He is allowed to deal with everything in us as we come to Him in faith. And if Jesus really is the same yesterday, as much as He is today and for ever (Heb. 13:8), we simply have to allow Him to help us conquer our past as much as He will our future.

We must not hold back anything; in this Advent season we must give Jesus room to walk backwards with us into our past. And He may do so with the support and expertise of others around us, but He will also do so through our quiet willingness to simply let Him walk into the dark horrors of our past.

Reflections on hope
- For some, 'more than a conqueror' is just Christian talk. It doesn't feel very real to them. How can we be more than winners when there are so many negative things going on around us and in our heads?
- What happens if the things we feel defeated by are linked to people in our past who are no longer alive? Surely we need to deal with the hurt because they can't do anything about it and we can't talk with them about the situation.

Creating space to act
Imagine: what would it be like to have nothing separating you from the love of Christ?

13 DEC

A new name for an old place

Bible text
Genesis 28:18–19

> Early the next morning Jacob took the stone he had placed under his head and set it up as a pillar and poured oil on top of it. He called that place Bethel, though the city used to be called Luz.

The book of Genesis is replete with make-overs. Names meant so much to ancient people, so there were numerous examples of people and places being re-branded. In this story Jacob is on the run from his brother Esau, who had vowed to kill him (Gen. 27:41). Esau's anger is understandable, for Jacob stole his spiritual blessing as the older twin. On his way to his uncle's home, Jacob stopped to rest under a tree in a place called Luz. The name meant 'to turn aside'.

As Jacob slept, God met with him in an amazing dream that effectively showed him his future prospects. He was to be the one through whom the ancient promise of future hope would be fulfilled. It seemed totally incongruous: a man who was running away from a life of treachery singled out for future blessing!

Jacob could not believe it. Suddenly this very ordinary place took on extraordinary meaning. Where he had spent the night with a stone for a pillow, God had changed his life and he had discovered that God could change his past as well as his future. He decided to call the spot 'the House of God'. Not everybody called it Bethel, in fact the name Luz was around for a very long time afterwards (Judg. 1:26), but for Jacob it became God's house for ever.

Doing hope

There is something very special about certain locations. Many of us will have special spots where very special things have taken place. In Los Angeles, California, there is a spot on which these words are written: 'Here the fire of God fell.' The words celebrate the place where the great revival of 1906 took place and sparked the birth of a worldwide Pentecostal movement.

People are usually standing somewhere when God shows up, and for all of us those places take on a very special meaning because they remind us of God's rush of hope in our time and space.

Many people can point to the very place where they met with God in their first conscious encounter with Him and experienced hope for the first time. Very often those places become monuments to the time and place when their past was changed and they experienced hope.

Increasingly, people of faith are linking geography to blessing. This is precisely why the land of Israel itself is such an important place. Having been to Israel on a number of occasions I never cease to be challenged, blessed and provoked by its testimony to what God has done in human history. Anyone who has been to Israel will understand why the land is called 'the fifth Gospel'. The place is inseparable from the Bible and our Christian understanding of hope.

But Advent also reminds us of its many challenges.

On a personal note, places sometimes need redeeming in our minds. They can become no-go areas where bad memories stalk us. When I first returned to the home in Jamaica, where I spent my first eight years, it was a very difficult experience. As I stood in the yard at my old home, where I experienced so many mixed emotions, I realised how much had changed in me.

Reflections on hope
- Places are important, but there is always a danger that we can become over sentimental in how we approach the business of spiritual geography. One such example may well be our approach to the land of Israel. What is a Christian response to the land of promise at this time of Advent?
- How does a place so filled with the promise of hope appear so hopeless given the political deadlock that stands at the centre of so much tension in our world today?

Creating space to act
Is there a place to which you need to return in order to redeem the memory of it?

14 DEC

A new name for a new man

Bible text
Genesis 32:26–28

> But Jacob replied, 'I will not let you go unless you bless me.'
> The man asked him, 'What is your name?'
> 'Jacob,' he answered.
> Then the man said, 'Your name will no longer be Jacob, but Israel, because you have struggled with God and with men and have overcome.'

When Jacob changed the name of a place from Luz to Bethel he was running away from his brother. In our verses today he is on his way back to meet his brother and is even more terrified.

The night before he was due to see his brother Esau, Jacob spent all night in an extended struggle with an angel. But it wasn't just a physical struggle – he was wrestling with his past. In order to do that he had to wrestle with his worst nightmares about himself.

After a long period the angel got to the core of the issue and asked for Jacob's name. His name was a hard thing to own up to: it meant 'cheater'. All his life he had lived up to it. He had been a shady character, swindling his way into his father's blessing with help from his mother (Gen. 27:5–40), though while living as a fugitive with his uncle Laban, the schemer was on the receiving end of Laban's deviousness.

So, the night before he had to reckon with his brother, Jacob had nothing to lose. To admit to his past was the final and most important step into a future of hope and promise. Now Jacob, the great name-changer, had *his* name changed by the angel. The new name meant the one who 'struggles with God', but there was no sense in which Jacob had beaten up the angel. Physically he came off worse, having earned himself a permanent limp in the process (Gen. 32:31). But he had struggled in the process to overcome with God's help.

Jacob walked away from that moment a different man.

Doing hope

My daughter told me recently that a church friend changed his name. Although he had known for some time that his name meant 'a small person', he finally decided that he could no longer live with it! So, while on a trip abroad, he told everyone that he was to be known by his family name. He is still a small person, but a change took place in his attitude towards himself.

Everyone who comes to faith in Christ lives in a world in which everything is made-over (2 Cor. 5:17). This 'make-over' must start with our attitudes towards ourselves. Hope for the past means we recognise that God has begun a new contract with us in which who we once were becomes secondary to who we are now supposed to be. Like Jacob all of us are on a journey, and although the Bible continued to call Jacob by the name he was given at birth, he was behaving more like Israel.

Some time ago I came across a prayer by an old black preacher: 'Lord I thank you that I ain't like I was but I ain't like I's gonna be!'

That's true for all of us.

Reflections on hope

- The interesting thing about our hope in Christ is that we may keep the same face but we change our nature. This is the marvel of our hope. However, it can be very confusing to be saints who still have the tendencies of sinners.
- The secret of our hope is that God still walks with us from the moment He promises to bless us to the time He fulfils His promises.
- Facing our past character can be quite traumatic, but it's worth the effort: the product is so much better.

Creating space to act

If there was one thing above everything else you could change about yourself, what would it be?

Hope for Today

The despair of hopelessness is our inability to see tomorrow because today we have no hope with which to live.

Advent is not just about Jesus, born to a virgin in a stable. It is about the baby who became a man and touched people who needed hope.

For many in Jesus' day hopelessness was about their sin and their need for a Saviour. But for many others it was about the snares in their everyday situations which stood in the way of the future.

In this week's studies from John's Gospel we meet five familiar individuals who were touched by Jesus' ministry. When He met them, hope came through spiritual renewal, but it also came through the freedom to think about a better life and a hope for today.

15 DEC

Starting over again

Bible text
John 3:7–10

> 'You should not be surprised at my saying, "You must be born again." The wind blows wherever it pleases. You hear its sound, but you cannot tell where it comes from or where it is going. So it is with everyone born of the Spirit.'
>
> 'How can this be?' Nicodemus asked.
>
> 'You are Israel's teacher,' said Jesus, 'and do you not understand these things?'

Under the cover of night a senior professor called Nicodemus came to Jesus for a theological debate. A teacher himself, he had been deeply impressed by Jesus' miracles and wanted to find out more. But he didn't expect the response he got from Jesus. Jesus told him that unless people experienced a rebirth they couldn't grasp the kingdom of God that Jewish people talked of and taught so much about (John 3:3).

The old professor didn't get it.

How on earth, he wondered, could an old man like himself be born all over again? Was he to make a re-entry into his mother's womb? His answer made it abundantly clear that he really didn't understand. Jesus explained that this birth 'from above' had nothing to do with physical procreation. It was entirely a spiritual reference. It was a new way of describing what happens when the human spirit is fused into the Spirit of God. As Jesus said, 'the Spirit gives birth to spirit' (John 3:6).

Every time Nicodemus opened his mouth his words tumbled out into questions. 'How can this be?' he pleaded. It was the same question the teenage virgin had asked the angel (Luke 1:34). Under the silence of the stars the old man was looking for hope. He was sincere enough, for it must have taken a great deal of humility for this prominent scholar to seek out a thirty-something rabbi for private tuition.

This passage, which gives us one of the clearest explanations of the concept of 'new birth', ends inconclusively: we don't know whether Nicodemus accepted Jesus' challenge. He certainly remained sympathetic and supportive (John 7:50–52; 19:39–40), but we have no clear evidence that he came to faith in Christ.

We do have clear evidence, however, that a serious paradigm shift took place for Nicodemus. He had to start all over again and think differently about life. This was the irony of Nicodemus' visit: an old teacher who failed to get the basics. What Nicodemus failed to grasp was that a hope-filled life began with a world-view which was itself birthed by God and that could not be man-made. Being 'born from above' was not an intellectual make-over but the radical renewal of the human spirit that takes us back to the meaning of life itself. This is eternal life.

Doing hope

Hope is the call to start over again. It's the challenge to 'unlearn' what life is all about. As Nicodemus discovered, it had nothing to do with material realities.

It should be no surprise to us if our non-Christian family and friends struggle to understand these things. As Paul reminds us, our natural instincts do not quickly grasp what faith is all about (1 Cor. 2:13–16). It is not natural to understand a concept of hope that begins with the idea of a baby born without any sexual contact between a man and a woman and who grew to teach and perform miracles, died on a cross and rose from death after three days. Entrance into Christian hope requires something far more radical than mere mental assent: it needs a rebirth of massive proportions.

The mystery of Advent is in itself a call to something entirely different. It asks people to make a giant leap, as they reach out, seek and find the living God. As we talk to people in search of hope we

need to be as open as Jesus was, remembering that starting all over
again is in itself a miracle.

Reflections on hope

- There is a great deal of talk about people who 'belong' to Christ
  before they believe in Christ. Which category would you put
  Nicodemus in? Was he a kind of believer or did he just stay on the
  edge of faith?
- What should we do about people who stay on the edge of
  Christian faith? Should we make attempts to pull them in or simply
  leave it up to God and the Holy Spirit? Or, is it possible that the
  Holy Spirit may use our push to pull them into the family of God?
- Over this Advent period greater numbers of people will come to
  our churches looking for hope. What does the story of Nicodemus
  have to offer us this Advent?

Creating space to act

For many of us it's been so long since we came to faith that we have
forgotten just what it means to have our minds renewed by hope.
For some it may have been a traumatic experience; for others it
was the gradual dawning of a new perspective. Remembering those
experiences may be the key to helping someone else make the same
journey of hope.

16 DEC

A thirst for life

Bible text
John 4:13–15

> Jesus answered, 'Everyone who drinks this water will be thirsty
> again, but whoever drinks the water I give him will never
> thirst ...'
> 'Sir, give me this water so that I won't get thirsty and have to
> keep coming here to draw water.'

Life in Jesus' day was filled with taboos. A very important one was that Jews did not associate with Samaritans. Another was that men didn't have social discourse with women unaccompanied.

As the Samaritan woman approached, Jesus asked for a drink. She was shocked and reminded Him of the cultural rule: Samaritans and Jews don't talk. But the conversation changed very rapidly and ended up as a discussion about water and eternal life.

It's hard to know if the woman really believed Jesus when He said that He would give her eternal life. The fact that she called Him 'Sir' could show that she wasn't being sarcastic. However, the conversation definitely shifted gear when Jesus told her about her serial relationships. The woman had had five husbands and her current relationship was also illegitimate (John 4:18). Before she knew it, they were talking about history, theology and hope.

Everybody else saw in her a woman with loose morals; a man-grabber. The very fact that she came alone to the well in the middle of the day was a tell-tale sign that this woman was probably an ostracised loner in her town. However, what Jesus saw was a woman looking for hope. In the conversation she discovered that this was the hope she had been looking for; this tired and thirsty Man by the well was the Messiah of whom all the prophets spoke, and she was having a one-to-one with Him!

The woman was so overwhelmed by the encounter that she left her water pot and ran off to tell everyone in her town about the Man who told her about her life (vv.28–29). What was really astounding was that the whole village wanted Him – a Jew – to spend time with them. Jesus spent two whole days with them (v.40).

A woman's thirst had been satisfied and she invited a whole town to get involved in the matter.

Doing hope

Most of us are on the lookout for something to give meaning to our lives. In this woman's case it seems likely that she was hungry for love and intimacy.

Many people rush after sexual gratification as the answer to their deepest needs. Sensuality defines their identity and provides a temporary inoculation from the bigger questions about their personal value and self-worth. To touch is to live, for a moment at least. And far too many of us measure our value by the things we possess. The scramble for a better life, which has resulted in excessive spending and hypermaterialism in our advanced economy, belies our true spiritual needs. We have far more millionaires today than we did two decades ago; people go abroad on holidays far more frequently; children wear designer clothes their parents only read about. Yet all the signs tell us that we are more restless and searching than we have ever been.

Life in Western society has become typified by a poverty of spirit that has not been with us in living memory, and for many millions the pain is in the empty expectations. Our growing gambling habits and indebtedness suggest that the hope we are seeking is always one gamble away. According to statistics, UK residents are 121 times more likely to be struck by lightning than they are to win £1m on the lottery!

There is nothing wrong with the pursuit of happiness. It has provoked and pushed many people into positive and fruitful lifestyles. But it should not be confused with the pursuit of hope, which is a far more important prize.

The thirst for life has been embedded in all of us. It is actually a sacred thirst and it refuses to be satisfied by anything of this world. If we are to fill our lives with meaning it is as profitable to fill a petrol tank with sand as it is to pour material things into the human spirit. Only lasting hope satisfies that thirst.

Reflections on hope

- There's nothing in this passage that tells us precisely when Jesus intended to open up a conversation with this woman. Was He there because she was coming or did He make use of the opportunity because she was there?
- Jesus soon got into a very meaningful conversation about the values by which this woman lived her life. How did He do this and what does it offer us as we attempt to become more involved with people from different cultures who are looking for hope?
- Once again, as we think about Advent and the spending spree that so often accompanies Christmas, how do we strike the right

balance between generosity and excess? Do we keep our cash or stretch our credit cards?

Creating space to act
Lord, so often I measure my value by what I have materially. Help me to see that my worth is found only in You. Amen.

17 DEC

Hope by proxy

Bible text
John 4:49–50

> The royal official said, 'Sir, come down before my child dies.' Jesus replied, 'You may go. Your son will live.'

Jesus was returning from His mission in Samaria and headed north into Cana. As He entered the town an official found Him and begged Him to travel further on to Capernaum to heal his son who was at the point of death. The boy had a raging fever.

Jesus didn't seem that impressed, however. He appeared in no hurry to get back to Capernaum. Perhaps He knew the boy would be dead by the time He got there. Maybe He was keen for him to stop suffering sooner rather than later. In any event, from some thirty kilometres away He ordered the boy's recovery and the fever stopped. Later the father learned that the fever left at exactly the same time Jesus told him it would (vv.52–53). The man's entire household became believers as a result of the miracle.

Jesus' behaviour exceeded the man's expectations. He expected Jesus to do something about his sick boy. That was the reason he had travelled so far to beg for his son's restoration. But what he hadn't figured was that Jesus had the ability to heal by proxy. Presumably he didn't realise that his request could trigger someone else's healing a long way away.

The man got a lot more than he came for.

Doing hope

Sometimes answers to our prayers are put on hold, and that can be difficult. But what makes hope such a potent gift in our circumstances is that God sometimes exceeds our expectations.

Recently, in a morning staff prayer meeting, we were asked to pray for people in other parts of the world, some of whom were going through persecution. We were also asked to pray for the families of four young men who had been murdered within a two-week period. I admitted afterwards that I felt a little overwhelmed by the set of circumstances we were confronted with. What hope was there that my prayers really would make any difference to these huge and intractable situations so far away?

But we know it works. We can pray and bring hope to others by proxy.

Many of us have experienced those moments when someone has told us that they were praying for us at a certain moment. That specific request, hundreds or even thousands of miles away, we know brought us hope and made a difference to our lives.

Hope can and does come by proxy as we stand on behalf of others to ask the Messiah for someone else's healing or exit route from their hopelessness. As the father in our reading found, it was worth the journey because his expectation brought hope to his dying son.

Reflections of hope

- The man had a vested interest in his child's healing. He was desperate because his child was desperate. Is it this desperation that activates God's response to our prayers for others? Casual prayers may betray the difference between formal duty when we 'remember' people in our prayers as opposed to agonising for them. People who walk long distances to stand in proxy for other people usually mean it.
- Sometimes we can feel distant from people we pray for as a matter of routine. How do we get beyond the distance that separates us in our prayers of hope for others?
- Can we really pray effectively for people we don't know at all? What difference does it make to our concern for them if we don't know them?

- This Advent will offer us many openings to pray for others who are a long way away. How will we seize those opportunities?

Creating space to act
Who is on your heart? Pray for them now.

18 DEC

A helping hand

Bible text
John 5:6–8

> When Jesus saw him lying there and learned that he had been in this condition for a long time, he asked him, 'Do you want to get well?'
>
> 'Sir,' the invalid replied, 'I have no-one to help me into the pool when the water is stirred. While I am trying to get in, someone else goes down ahead of me.'
>
> Then Jesus said, 'Get up! Pick up your mat and walk.'

The poor man was so near and yet so very far. Although we have no idea how long he had been coming to the pool, he had been an invalid for thirty-eight years. It was a very long time. So, there was a good deal of desperation in this man's life.

The pool was a very unusual one, for it seemed that every so often it would be stirred up, releasing healing properties – but only enough to heal one person at a time.

When Jesus came along it became evident that the man had been there for a very long time, so the question Jesus asked him was very strange indeed. Did he want to get well? It must have been obvious to everybody. Why else would the man stay by the edge of the pool waiting to be first in?

It was a deliberate and calculated question. Jesus often asked people if they wanted to get well because a healing meant more than getting better; it meant a change of lifestyle. Cripples and blind men who were healed were no longer candidates for begging. It meant independence: taking responsibility for themselves. But the man said a lot more than 'Yes'; He gave a whole explanation. He had no one to help him in. Other people always beat him to it because the nature of his complaint meant he was a slow starter. Perhaps he didn't know about Jesus' reputation as a healer, so direct healing was not on the agenda.

He needed a helping hand: someone willing enough to stay until the pool was stirred to push him in at the right time. Instead, Jesus told him to get up, take up his mat and walk. And he did.

I would like to have met this man. Anyone crippled for so long who made a special effort against the odds must have been very courageous. If you had no one to help you and saw others beat you to the pool over a long period of time it would take an act of huge desperation and tenacity to keep coming back. But he did. The nature of his complaint and the fact that he had no help gave him the perfect excuse not to bother. He knew that without help he would never get into the pool in time, but he never gave up trying. He wasn't looking for favours: he wanted help.

Doing hope

Hope comes in many different parcels.

Two years ago I had the privilege of visiting India with the Christian charity World Vision. We went to see the work that had been done there after the 2004 tsunami. There, again and again, I saw hope. Hope was a red tractor in the middle of a field; a fishing boat and a cow in a yard owned by a mother and her three children.

Hope is the story of countless thousands of young people who have taken time out of their studies to travel across the world in order to give their time and energies to people they have never met. A gap year is a helping hand and an offer of hope.

We have no way of knowing what the crippled man's relationship to God was, but when Jesus met him his hope was his physical healing. Jesus made no mention of sin as he did on other occasions (Mark 2:5).

Sometimes it is enough that people around us experience a God of hope when they are given a helping hand. There is no contradiction here: the good news about hope is supremely the news that our sins are forgiven. But it is not the only news about good news.

Christian witness has always included acts of hope as well as statements *about* hope.

Reflections on hope
- Every Advent gives us excellent opportunities to offer people a helping hand. How might this work for you or your local fellowship?
- With relatively little effort it's possible to find a myriad of ways in which we can give a helping hand to thousands of people who need it – both at home and abroad.
- Admittedly, not everyone makes good use of our help. Jesus passed a lot of other people by the pool who also needed help, but He was rather selective on this occasion. How might we identify the people who will maximise our help?

Creating space to act
If you listen keenly enough you may find that those who need a helping hand are not that far away. Or you may need to buy a ticket to somewhere else.

19 DEC

A better way to live

Bible text
John 8:10–11

> Jesus straightened up and asked her, 'Woman, where are they? Has no-one condemned you?'
> 'No-one, sir,' she said.
> 'Then neither do I condemn you,' Jesus declared. 'Go now and leave your life of sin.'

When the teachers of the law and the Pharisees brought this woman to Jesus it was a very serious matter.

It was serious for the woman because it really was a matter of life and death. But as she stood there on the edge of death, it was also serious for Jesus because He knew that the challenge was also directed at Him and His approach to the Law of Moses. If He endorsed the stoning He would become like the Pharisees – more interested in Law than in grace. But if He stopped them carrying out the Law He would have brought about His own premature death.

This is one of the most startling examples of how Jesus balanced grace and truth. This was John's great introduction of the Messiah (John 1:14,17). Hope balances grace and truth in perfect and delicate harmony. Jesus did not rush into judgment. In fact, His slow response annoyed the onlookers (v.7). He was in no rush to condemn the woman. But He also included everyone in her personal sin. If the stone throwers had no sin, He suggested that they should begin the execution there and then. They couldn't go ahead with it. Suddenly everybody became overwhelmed by their own sin and lost sight of the woman's adultery. Sin became a communal reality.

Finally, Jesus stood to ask where the execution squad was. They had all gone, said the woman. No one brought any condemnation. Jesus decided He would not condemn her either. He could have given her a lecture and she would have been obliged to pay attention, but she already knew how wrong she was. She had been caught red-handed, and the pile of stones nearby was reminder enough. But neither would Jesus condone the woman's sin. He did, however, want her to know that there was a better way to live. Go home – you can do better than that, he told her.

Plucked from her lover's bed she had been brought out into public to die, but instead she was given a hope to live by.

Doing hope

Christians have a very serious view of sin and this is precisely why Advent is so important to us. Jesus came not to give us presents but to forgive our sin. And for believers more than anyone else this Advent season draws an unbroken line between the terrible reality of the Fall (Gen. 3) and the hope of redemption because of the cross of Jesus. This is quintessentially the Christmas story. It is the story of hope.

Advent is God's story of how God's Law was met by His response of grace in the birth, ministry, death and resurrection of Jesus Christ.

It is so easy to rush into judgment in the name of truth. For too many of us Christians our major mission is to remind the world of its sin. It is to be in opposition to everyone else, crying out against our culture with strident tones of condemnation. But that is not the tone of Advent. At Advent Jesus came to live with us (John 1:14). In the Advent account there is a tenderness we would do well to recreate.

This grace is also truthful enough to point out everybody's sins and sinfulness. Our private sins are important to God. He is offended by them. But He is also outraged by our corporate sins. It is far easier to point the finger – to advertise our neighbour's sin and the misdemeanours of our public figures – but it is far more important to recognise how much all of us become implicated in each other's sins.

Finally, though, we should give people hope.

At the height of the troubles in Northern Ireland, a Christian leader led worship immediately after a major bombing incident in London. Her prayer was very powerful. 'Lord,' she said, 'we pray for the terrorists. Give them a better idea of how to live.'

And that is the hope we offer: a better way to live.

People in the twenty-first century need to hear that reconciliation gives them a better way to live.

Reflections on hope

- It's not easy to blend grace and truth: it's far easier to emphasise one over and against the other. We don't really have an option, however, because it's what Jesus did.
- How did Jesus dwell among us without condemning us? Surely He had a lot to say about sin and punishment. Aren't we in danger of losing the impact of Advent if we lose sight of this?
- Does Advent give us any opportunities to speak into unjust issues? How should we approach this?

Creating space to act

Lord, help me to keep the right balance of grace in my relationships with others. Amen.

20 DEC

Seeing clearly

Bible text
John 9:10–11

'How then were your eyes opened?' they demanded.

He replied, 'The man they call Jesus made some mud and put it on my eyes. He told me to go to Siloam and wash. So I went and washed, and then I could see.'

As Jesus walked along with His disciples He saw this man who had been born blind. His condition opened up a discussion about his blindness: was he blind because he had sinned in a previous life or was it because of something his parents had done? One way or another, someone was to be blamed. Jesus explained that his blindness had nothing to do with the man or his parents. God wanted to bring hope to someone who wasn't asking for it (John 9:3). It was to be an object lesson in how important light is.

So, after Jesus spat on the ground, made mud and put it on the man's eyes, He had him struggle off to the pool of Siloam. Then the man discovered he could see.

The man must have had moments, however, when he wondered if it was worth the hassle. Being born blind he would have been accustomed to a world of darkness; he was hardly ready for the controversy that accompanied his gift of sight. The whole debate got so bad that the man who gained his sight eventually lost his place in the community (v.34).

No one celebrated with him. His parents distanced themselves from the debate for fear of the authorities, the people who knew him spent more time discussing his identity rather than showing gratitude and the authorities saw it as another opportunity to have Jesus killed.

What the ex-blind man saw was that people who don't want to believe will always find an excuse for their unbelief! If it wasn't a matter of identity it became issues around Sabbath-keeping. He found too that even close relatives might desert you and leave you with your happy story if their lives or livelihoods are at stake. He saw that people who had sight couldn't see when God was at work and that blindness is also a spiritual condition of the heart.

He learned that not everyone embraces hope, even when it is freely available. He discovered that scepticism can kill hope.

Doing hope

I was preparing for a television interview and was sharing the greenroom with an eminent atheist. True to form he was rubbishing the concept of God. He said that there was no scientific proof of God's existence: God was a great illusion and this was why he was an atheist.

I asked what it would take to convince him conclusively that God existed. He thought for a moment and said that if an audible voice came from the roof of the studio and called out to him then he 'might conceivably' believe. But almost as quickly he destroyed his own example by providing a plausible explanation as to why an audible voice might occur! So, I said, if there was no conclusive scientific proof to demonstrate that God did exist, could he produce any conclusive scientific evidence that God does not exist? He couldn't think of any. In which case, I suggested, he could not really be an atheist and at best could only be an agnostic. 'I suppose so,' he conceded.

It was scepticism not science that kept this man away from hope.

We should not be shaken when God reaches out in hope only to have it rejected. It's quite incredible: in the glaring light of amazing miracles people may still choose hopelessness. As John said, Jesus came to His very own, who chose darkness instead of light (1:11).

Reflections on hope

- Miracles don't always convince people that hope has arrived. It is in the very nature of darkness to choose the dark and to shut out hope.
- Our blindness can come in degrees. How do we protect ourselves from spiritual black-outs?
- Jim Wallis, the American Christian activist and writer, once said that the real battle is not between truth and falsehood but between hope and scepticism. Is he right?

Creating space to act

It was quite some time before I realised that I was becoming shortsighted. I didn't realise until other schoolboys were reading the numbers on the front of buses and pushing to the front of the queue long before I did.

21 DEC

Living again

Bible text
John 11:25–26

> Jesus said to her, 'I am the resurrection and the life. He who believes in me will live, even though he dies; and whoever lives and believes in me will never die. Do you believe this?'

There is nothing more final than death. That is why funerals are such deeply sobering events. The finality accompanying death is deeply moving because in the realisation of this terminal condition each of us is confronted by our own mortality. Because death can never be delegated to someone else, no one can experience it for another person.

By the time Jesus arrived in Bethany His good friend Lazarus had been dead for four days. It was bad enough having to wait for him to die, but to walk the gauntlet of his sisters' distress just made the whole thing so much more painful. Even as He explained to Mary and Martha, Jesus knew that they were unable to hear what He was saying through the pain. Even as they made their way to the tomb no one expected to see Lazarus again. It was all too late: Jesus really should have come earlier (John 11:32).

But four days was about right for what Jesus had in mind. There could be no question that this was a trick. The stench was terrible. After four days, decomposition had set in and decomposition was nature's way of saying that the situation was hopeless. By then there was no way of claiming that Lazarus was in a coma. He really had gone. For good.

Everybody thought that Jesus cried because He loved Lazarus so much (v.36). But it was something else. It was probably the horror of death itself and the recognition that before too long He Himself would enter it in the most awful way. But when He shouted at Lazarus, hope ran riot through the corpse. The dead man emerged from the tomb (v.44).

Doing hope

Nothing demonstrates Jesus' ability to solve the unsolvable like this story. It was God's way of saying that He has the ability to deal with the final assault on hope. If a man can be retrieved from death then there is no limit to God's ability to resuscitate life in our dead situations.

This is also extremely important for Christian hope. It means that God makes the possibility of physical restoration very possible indeed. We should believe in God's ability to heal our physical bodies.

It means too that if God can resurrect a body after four days He can also do it after 400 years! This miracle of resurrection pointed forward to Jesus' own experience, but much more, it points forward to the Christian teaching about the resurrection of our own physical bodies (1 Cor. 15:12–58).

Reflections on hope

- At what point do you suppose Mary and Martha realised what Jesus was about to do?
- How would you explain Jesus' incredible emotions? There are only two places in the Bible where Jesus cried, and this was one of them.
- A story like this should encourage us to pray for God's healing and wholeness in our physical sicknesses, but does God still raise dead people today? Why He would do so?

Creating space to act

'Where, O death, is your victory?
Where, O death, is your sting?'
The sting of death is sin, and the power of sin is the law. But thanks be to God! He gives us the victory through our Lord Jesus Christ.
Therefore, my dear brothers, stand firm. Let nothing move you.
(1 Cor. 15:55–58)

WEEK FOUR
Hope to Live By

When Jesus eventually appeared on the scene, the promise of thousands of years materialised in the life experiences of a wide range of people. Some of them expected it. Others were taken by surprise.

This week's study pulls back the curtain on some of the key characters in the Advent story and what the arrival of hope meant for them.

For Mary and Joseph, Elizabeth and Zechariah, the hope of the nations became a personal experience that pulled them in and changed their lives forever. This realised hope of the Messiah was highly inconvenient. For the shepherd it was a reminder that God includes the uninvited. For a faithful old man – Simeon – and a very old prophetess – Anna – it was a case of patience and prayer rewarded.

Hope alive!

Bible text
Luke 1:11–13

> Then an angel of the Lord appeared to him, standing at the
> right side of the altar of incense. When Zechariah saw him, he
> was startled and was gripped with fear. But the angel said to
> him: 'Do not be afraid, Zechariah; your prayer has been heard.
> Your wife Elizabeth will bear you a son ...'

When I was a Bible student, chapel attendance was a regular part of
student life. It was a privilege but it could also become a chore. One
day a lecturer prayed a very important prayer I shall never forget.
'Lord protect us,' he said 'from the apparatus of regular worship.' It
was a very honest and a very real prayer.

There's always the danger that even our most sacred worship
can become nothing more than a duty, and even our most earnest
prayers can become predictable requests without hope.

Zechariah was in danger of that. As a priest his duties would
have been meticulously repetitive. Sacred lines would have
become familiar. The rituals would have routines. As a priest
he was also charged with the responsibility of the spiritual
health of the whole community. Priests were intercessors for
everyone's relationship with Yahweh. The nation's spiritual life
was inconceivable without his prayers. This was 'the custom of the
priesthood' (Luke 1:9).

Familiarity is one thing, but when we are programmed to pray
for everybody else it's easy to fall into an auto-ministry in which we

disappear as individuals. That is the place where hope becomes hollow.

But, on that day, hope came alive for the priest who turned up to the Temple to do what he had done a thousand times before. At long last God's plans for the arrival of the Saviour were about to be enacted, and an integral part of the plan would be the priest's son. Praying for the Messiah would have been a familiar act for this man, but he would never have guessed that his own prayers for a child would be the opening scene of the Messiah's arrival! His private prayers became public property. That day, beyond the rituals of his duty, hope was coming alive.

It was all too much for the man who lived by talking. Just when he got the most exciting news ever he lost his voice (v.20)!

Doing hope

The easiest thing in the world is to talk and sing about our hope in Christ and yet to know little of its truth.

Like Zechariah, most of us go through the motions. We walk through the routine of sermon preparations, leading our youth groups or even our daily devotions, as mere duty. In too many instances our Sunday experiences provide us with little variety beyond the monotony of repeated songs and formats which offer very little substance that's new. Even our Advent celebrations may be in danger of becoming annual rituals rather than a celebration of our lively hope.

Our worship and work should be replenished by our living hope. Can you imagine what the Temple would have felt like for Zechariah on his subsequent duties? In our prayers, worship and work we should live as though hope has come! This truth should make all the difference to monotony.

In God's goodness He will often find us in the routine and remind us that our prayers are not forgotten. And like a child we should keep an expectant eye open when we pray.

Reflections on hope

- Zechariah was just doing his work as a priest when hope came alive for him. So does this mean, therefore, that God can only renew our hope if we are in church? What examples do we have to tell about God breaking into our routine in other places giving us renewed hope?

- What should we do about creating environments that reduce predictable routine, and does God really care about these things anyway? Isn't there something already very powerful and Spirit-filled in our liturgies and daily routines? In fact, God has more routines than anyone else, and built them into the Bible. He must be at work in them even when we are not aware of it – as Zechariah discovered.

- If we are all priests before God we have a responsibility to take the needs of our world to God – especially during this Advent season. How easy is it to pray meaningfully about the needs of our world and also balance our own needs?

Creating space to act

Strangely, when Zechariah had the biggest testimony ever he was struck dumb. But think how much more intense that hope became in the silence; how much deeper he had to internalise it; and how much more powerful and convincing it was when he finally blurted it out.

Sometimes hope gestates quietly before anyone else knows about it.

23 DEC

Hope in hiding

Bible text
Luke 1:24–25

> After this his wife Elizabeth became pregnant and for five months remained in seclusion. 'The Lord has done this for me,' she said. 'In these days he has shown his favour and taken away my disgrace among the people.'

Christians have become great at marketing God. We spend millions on promotion. It's only natural, therefore, that we jump to the conclusion that a successful ministry is high-profile and televised and that anything which offers hope for the nation belongs on a public platform.

That was not Elizabeth's take on hope.

When Zechariah discovered that he and Elizabeth were destined to become ageing parents, his speech had been taken from him by the angel Gabriel (Luke 1:20). When Elizabeth became pregnant she retreated into silence. No fanfare or press releases – just self-imposed isolation. Her fulfilled dream of becoming a mother threw her into a curious tension. Her son John was to become the forerunner of the Messiah and her acute embarrassment as a barren woman was being terminated. But only at further cost, for the sight of a mother-to-be 'well on in years' (v.7) would have provoked as much gossip as a childless woman.

Silence and anonymity was the only solution to her good news. Not too much energy wasted in lengthy explanations and overt stares in the village high street. But there was no resentment. No extended questions about why God waited so long: only overwhelming joy that her hope had been rewarded. As Elizabeth said, 'The Lord has done this …' (v.25).

And the Lord knew that it would not be convenient for Elizabeth and Zechariah. When God fulfilled their hope He knew that it would push them into silent awkwardness. God was fully aware that they would have a story that could not be told at once and that hope would be silent before it became a song. When Elizabeth broke silence it was to celebrate with Mary (vv.42–45). And when Zechariah was allowed to speak again it came out in song (vv.67–79).

This is very important. Elizabeth could have been arrogant enough to cope with the taunts and flaunt her blessing. After all, she was used to being the talk of the town – why not really give the gossipers something to talk about and declare herself a graduate from the company of barren women?

Before their hope became public it went underground. Elizabeth and Zechariah knew something no one else on earth yet knew, and they both decided to go into hiding with it. And when they emerged it wasn't to draw attention to themselves, it was to point everyone to what God had done.

Doing hope

During the Cultural Revolution in China, Christians virtually disappeared. We have no idea how many lives have been lost over the past four decades.

Over the past twenty years, however, Christians have been talking about the 'underground church' in China. Today no one knows quite how many millions form that powerful movement of God's people there. As the accounts of the Chinese Church trickle out, what is clear is the extent to which it has been silent in hope. There is little doubt that over the next two decades Christians in places that were formerly silent in hope will play a dominant role in the growth of Christian faith in Western societies.

That should be an encouragement to all of us. Hope does not always come with a fanfare. In our lives and ministries God will often prepare and commission us in quiet places. In many instances anonymity will precede popularity. There will also be many more of us who may never rise to public platforms but who, nonetheless, will be great ministers of hope. As a preacher said recently, success is not necessarily about big breaks: it's about lots of little people with big dreams who work together to resist the poverty of hope in other people's lives.

Being silent in hope can be tough, but often this is precisely what God wants from us. For, it is often in the silence that we are best prepared to cope with the clamour of the people who have no hope and to whom we are sent.

Hope is powerful because it is real – not just because everybody knows about it.

Reflections on hope

- Why on earth should Elizabeth hide herself from other people, just at the time when she would have a fantastic testimony? Surely it would be a much stronger witness to show up old and pregnant and give people a chance to see the pregnancy develop. Her neighbours may have thought that she'd adopted if she just re-appeared with a new baby at her age!
- The Bible says we should be ready to tell people about the hope we have within us (1 Pet. 3:15) and we are warned not to hide our lights under a covering (Matt. 5:14–16). So why are there times

when we should we keep hope quiet? It sounds like something of a contradiction. Are we talking here about the hope of faith in Christ or something else?

Creating space to act
How quiet can you be? Pray through what you have read today and ask God to speak to you. Stop and listen.

24 DEC

Hope and horrors

Bible text
Luke 1:28–30

> The angel went to her and said, 'Greetings, you who are highly favoured! The Lord is with you.'
> Mary was greatly troubled at his words and wondered what kind of greeting this might be. But the angel said to her, 'Do not be afraid, Mary, you have found favour with God.'

There is an idea that when God covers us with favour all our fears and problems disappear. If you mentioned that theory to Mary, however, she would have fallen off her stool with laughter.

On the day when the angel appeared, Mary was busy getting on with what appeared to be an uneventful life. Something about her character, though, had already attracted God and today she was singled out for a very special mission. She was to bring the Messiah into the world.

But from the moment the angel appeared her life was filled with fear. It wasn't just that angels tended to be somewhat imposing beings. There is nothing in the story to suggest that the angel made her jump. What made her fearful and anxious was what he said about her future (v.29). She just couldn't be sure what this unprecedented greeting meant. And with good reason – what did it mean to have God's favour? The angel explained: she was to be the

Messiah's mum (v.32)!

This was not a comfortable thing to hear. In a moment Mary rummaged through the implications in her mind. She was due to be married to Joseph: what would her neighbours – never mind her family – make of such a thing? In any event, how was she to become pregnant without having had sex? In addition to all of this, the vision the angel brought to her was huge! An everlasting kingdom? The throne of David? It was all too much.

From this point and for the next thirty-three years Mary lived out the full implications of this moment in embarrassment and wonder. She lived through the stigma of Jesus' parental status; she gave away her Son to the world and stood by to watch Him die for the sins of people she would never meet.

Mary was full of joy, but her Christmas was not very merry.

Sometimes hope comes with horrors.

Advent is not a Disney wonderland. It's a harsh and powerful reminder that hope often comes at a price.

Doing hope

For a growing number of Christians there is a definition of Christian hope that is most frequently associated with material blessings. And it is precisely at this time of the year that many of us are tempted to measure God in material terms as we merge into the commercial streams flowing together into what we call 'the Christmas spirit'. Many believe in a God who prospers us materially; who heals our bodies and responds to our prayers by attending to our needs.

But, even more, we should believe in a hope that is alive and powerful in the midst of our problems and fears. Hope is not incompatible with horror but it never caves in to it. Invariably our hope stirs up the horrors of the night. For only by hoping for great things from God do we become aware of the size of the enterprise in which we are involved and our inability to do anything about it on our own. Perhaps if we are not horrified by what hope provokes us to become, we have not properly understood God's intentions in the world.

Hope for today never makes us afraid but gives us permission to be overwhelmed by the enormity of what God has in mind. That's when hope is at its best in our world.

Reflections on hope

- There is a lot of sense in the idea that people who come to faith in Christ should prosper and live more successful lives than anyone else. This makes for good witness because at the end of the day people want to belong to something that offers visible benefits. What's the good of Christian faith if it has no fringe benefits? Doesn't this make God superior to other gods? Discuss.
- If Mary's experience was so horrific, her great song of praise makes no sense (Luke 1:46–55). Presumably she got over the initial shock and everything worked out from then on. What do you think?
- If we have a sense that a mission is overwhelming, it is bound to leave us shell-shocked. God must surely be looking for fearless people who will take on anything the twenty-first century can throw at us. Fear gets in the way of faith and makes us spiritual pigmies in the land of giants. Do you agree?

Creating space to act

Lord, with Christmas close at hand, help me to resist the material and commercial aspects of the season. Help me to focus on You above all else. Amen.

25 DEC

Hope and the ego-free servant

Bible text
Luke 2:3–4

> And everyone went to his own town to register.
> So Joseph also went up from the town of Nazareth in Galilee to Judea, to Bethlehem the town of David, because he belonged to the house and line of David.

In the average Christmas nativity play nobody pays much attention to Joseph. Usually the sheep and oxen get a bigger laugh!

However, Joseph was a central character in the drama of the Saviour. Joseph, a 'righteous man', also had some tough choices to make. He couldn't quite believe Mary's account at first, and until the angel spoke to him personally (Matt. 1:19–21) it seemed that the proper thing to do was to abandon the wedding plans. It must have taken a lot for this man to walk into the entire episode supporting Mary through her trauma and excitement when he had his own problems to work through. What were people going to say about this baby? How would he explain it to his parents and what would this all say about his masculinity?

Joseph was far from passive. He was an active, ego-free contributor to the programme of hope. It was to Joseph that the angel came to plot the escape to Egypt and return journey back to Israel (Matt. 2:13,19–20). And we should not forget that Jesus was born in Bethlehem, not because of Mary, but because of Joseph. It was Joseph's lineage – not Mary's – through which the unbroken lineage to David was made (Matt. 1:16; Luke 2:4).

Joseph had more encounters with angels than anyone else in this drama. And more than anyone else he seemed quite at home with them: three encounters and no sign of being overwhelmed. But he needed to hear from angels for himself. Mary's account would not be enough. Within his culture he was still the man in his home and God had no plans to take that responsibility away from him. But he also needed his own assurances. His strength would be Mary's support and Jesus' safety.

Hope would have been inconceivable without Joseph's selfless love.

Doing hope

I can still remember what it felt like to pace the corridors of the maternity ward as I awaited the birth of my son. Fathers were included somewhat more by the time my daughter came along two years later, but even then I had the feeling of being surplus to requirements as all the action happened around my wife. She was rightly the centre of attention.

But apparently what little I did was a big help!

There are times when what is most required is a supporting role. The importance of a cool head and an unpretentious willingness to stand with the main character should never be underestimated. Sometimes we are only directed to do what helps someone else in his or her work, and the greatest and most effective ministry is to play a supporting role.

Indeed, the best partnerships in ministry usually work well because someone is prepared to offer a great back-up support ministry. As one minister told me, 'I'm called to be the best number two there can be!'

When we need to be, a supporting act is the best role there is.

Reflections on hope

- Like everywhere, churches can be places where egos run riot and good people get abused. All of us have a responsibility to hear what God is saying about our role. If God calls you to serve someone else don't worry if others feel you are a pushover. If you haven't had a very clear calling in this regard it's always good to check the dynamic of a supportive role if it feels uncomfortable.
- Hope comes through many players. Service is not the role of the underdog. It requires great strength and an ego-free attitude to do God's work.
- If you are called as a leader of any kind it's always worth checking how you support those who support you. When does service look like abuse? And how much does their service to you release them to be what God has called them to be?

Creating space to act

I imagine Mary would have said 'thank you' to Joseph a thousand times throughout the years. How about you? Have you said 'thank you' to those who have supported you in your life?

26 DEC

Hope on the night shift

Bible text
Luke 2:8–10

> And there were shepherds living out in the fields near by,
> keeping watch over their flocks at night. An angel of the Lord
> appeared to them, and the glory of the Lord shone around
> them, and they were terrified. But the angel said to them, 'Do
> not be afraid. I bring you good news of great joy …'

As a shepherd in the first century you would have been somewhere
towards the bottom end of the economic food chain. To be a
shepherd was lowly enough, but to be a shepherd on the night shift
was an even poorer deal. And to be a shepherd on the night shift in
an Israel occupied by the Romans meant that a visitation of angels
was the last thing you would have expected to happen on your
watch!

So an angel turning up, followed by an entire gospel choir (Luke
2:13), was destined to be told as a party-piece for years to come.

For these people hope came in the normality of a late shift
keeping wolves at bay. The shift called for special vigilance and
attentiveness, but for the shepherd it was all in a night's work. It's
worth noting too that the shepherds weren't just passing through
the countryside. This was where they lived: they were country boys
(v.8).

It was here, though, that the glory of God came. Not among the
religious leaders or the chattering classes in Jerusalem, and definitely
not in Herod's palace! Zechariah had been visited in the Temple and
now here in the open field during the night watch God shared the
most stupendous news with a group of unsuspecting shepherds on
whom His glory fell.

Through their terror and fear they discovered that God was
directing shepherds to become messengers – 'good news agents' to
the town of Bethlehem (v.17)! It's highly probable that these men
suddenly found an audience among people who would not normally

spend time with them.

Good news crosses barriers.

Doing hope

So often we think of finding God's purposes in unusual places. People travel to many special sites or visit special conferences and residential settings to find God. Many of us have spent small fortunes chasing illusive blessings. There must be a place for all of that, but God can find us and send us rushing off into unknown adventures while we are doing the most ordinary things.

David du Plessis was a powerful and influential Pentecostal pioneer whose ministry reached way beyond the Pentecostal movement of his day. Like the shepherds in the fields, he was also sent to take good news to people beyond his own social setting. In his autobiography, *A Man Called Mr Pentecost*, he tells of a very important discovery about God's ability to work in the mundane. It was a lesson he learned from his wife.

He began to notice remarkable changes in his wife's behaviour. One day he watched her closely as she was ironing and noticed that she actually loved spending time at the ironing board.

Let him tell us in his own words:

'Oh' she said, 'this is the time when I don't need to do anything but talk to the Lord. I can iron and talk. It's fun.'

Her chores had become pleasures because of the freedom Jesus had given us. While her hands were going a mile a minute, she prayed for me, for the children, for the brethren, for whomever the Lord put on her mind. She and I both had taken the first steps toward living by prayer, not by the law, not by the clock, not by a formula. It came through talking to the Lord all the time, anytime, anywhere.

If He were to say, 'Saskatchewan,' we were ready to go to Saskatchewan, although we hadn't the slightest idea where it was.[1]

At Advent good news came first to very ordinary people, and it is still the case that most of the work of God is done through so-called

---

1. David du Plessis, *A Man Called Mr Pentecost* (Logos International, 1977), p.59.

ordinary people He meets in the ordinary tasks to which they are called. Usually it's from here that we are sent to do extraordinary things and take a message of hope to people who might not otherwise listen to us.

Reflections on hope
- There are still a lot of Christians who are convinced that only people doing 'Christian ministry' really count. What counts though is not where we are but how closely we listen to what God is saying to us.
- Don't go looking for boring things to do though! There is no special virtue in it. Most jobs have the equivalent of their night shifts. The point is that God can reach us on the night shift – whatever we're doing and wherever we are.
- For some people the 'night shift' could be another way of talking about those periods in our ministries where we feel that we are marking time or going through a particular time of vulnerability. The question always arises: can God see well enough in the dark to notice I'm there?

Creating space to act
How do you practise the presence of God where you are?

27 DEC

Hope fulfilled

Bible text
Luke 2:29–32

> Sovereign Lord, as you have promised,
>   you now dismiss your servant in peace.
> For my eyes have seen your salvation,
>   which you have prepared in the sight of all people,
> a light for revelation to the Gentiles
>   and for glory to your people Israel.

In his heart the old man cherished one thing above everything else: the day when he would see the Messiah for himself. His name was Simeon, and whenever he talked about the Messiah there was something very different about what he had to say. His study of the Messiah was not academic: it was personal. He was less concerned about the technical details of the genealogies or the finer points about the exact location where the Messiah would be born. Others could worry about that. He had one abiding conviction and it was the lens through which he worshipped and watched for the Saviour. He had been promised a personal audience before he died.

He attached no national importance to this promise. In the greater scheme of things it would decide nothing. As far as he could see, it had no far-reaching impact. It was simply that God, by the Holy Spirit made a personal promise that he would see the Saviour of Israel (Luke 2:26). Simeon lived every day for nothing else and he was quite prepared to die having done so.

He lived in Jerusalem, so he visited the Temple often. But on this particular day that same compelling voice of the Holy Spirit told him to set off for the Temple (v.27). He was the only one who didn't need an angel to tell him what was taking place. When he arrived he saw a couple consecrating a new baby. He knew at once that this was the child he was promised to see. This was the 'consolation of Israel' (v.25).

He took the boy in his arms – his parents were happy to trust the old man – and blessed Him. They were taken aback not just by the incredible words he prayed; it was also the intensity in his prayer. They watched their new baby in the arms of the old man and knew it was a matter of life and death for him.

When Simeon walked out into the sunlight he had nothing left to live for.

Doing hope

Waiting for hope is hard but really important. In a world where we are so programmed to act, waiting runs counter to our culture. John Milton's powerful *Sonnet on His Blindness* captures this reality very well. From the relative speed of his own day he reminds us that: 'They also serve who only stand and wait.'

Waiting tempers the human spirit and gives us time to confront our self and the values by which we live. Simeon knew what was important to him and he devoted himself to it. It governed his prayers and worship and dominated his concept of the meaning of his life.

Hope for today is never dependent on our efforts alone. We are always a part of a team reaching back to the very dawn of Abraham's faith and reaching forward to the unknown future. God will always applaud our faith, patience and activism, but He is also impressed when we know we have run our race.

In the same way that we in the present fulfil the hopes of those who came before us (Heb. 11:39–40) we must know that God's programme will never finish with us. God often calls other people to make our prayers come to pass.

In his sobering work, *Reflections on the Revolution in France*, Edmund Burk expresses similar sentiments like this:

> As the ends of such a partnership cannot be obtained in many generations it becomes a partnership not only between those who are living but between those who are living, those who are dead and those who are to be born.[1]

This realisation allows us to hold things lightly and to let things go at the right time. It reassures us that however faithful we have been in our time, God's Advent of hope is only dependent on us to do what we have been called to do. Others will come behind us.

Knowing this helps us to 'hand the baby back'.

Reflections on hope
- It can be so hard to wait. What makes it something of an ordeal is the danger of mistaking waiting for inactivity.
- Simeon had the balance right: he possessed his hope without being possessive about it. How do we do that with the things God has given us to do?
- How resilient do we think hope is and how easy might we find it to let go when we need to do so?

---

1. Edmund Burk, *Reflections on the Revolution in France* (Oxford University Press, 1999).

Creating space to act

Lord, help me to know when it is time to move on. If it is now, please show me what I must do next. Amen.

28 DEC

Hope for a Temple-dweller

Bible text

Luke 2:36–37

> There was also a prophetess, Anna, the daughter of Phanuel, of the tribe of Asher. She was very old; she had lived with her husband seven years after her marriage, and then was a widow until she was eighty-four. She never left the temple but worshipped night and day, fasting and praying.

Some people appear very briefly in Scripture to make a deep impression on us before receding into the pages again. Anna is one such person. Everything about her was non-descript. A descendant of Asher, she would have had no real cultural significance as the tribe had long ceased to be a reference point in Israel's history. They had no inheritance at all.

Her life was in many ways something of a disaster. She wasn't just old, she was 'very old'; few people in the Bible are described like that. After only seven years of marriage, her husband died leaving her to widowhood for more than half a century. Whether Anna retreated into a monastic lifestyle or felt called to it is difficult to tell. But it's quite clear that all of her interests became absorbed into the life of the Temple. Prayer and fasting, worship and waiting, she was on standby for the appearance of the Messiah. What might have been a very lonely life became a very focused one.

On the same day that old Simeon was deliberately directed to the Temple, Anna was on hand to join in the celebrations.

Anna's lifestyle is not for everyone! However, she is a model of focused devotion whose lifestyle was rewarded beyond her wildest dreams. I suspect if you asked Anna whether her life of sacrifice was worth that one moment she would shout a resounding 'Yes!'

Doing hope

Life doesn't always treat us favourably. Anna's long status as a widow would not have been her first choice. We can only imagine that the fact that she came from an obscure tribe meant that her chances of remarrying were very slim.

However, if we are trapped in adverse circumstances we still have a choice. We can implode, folding in on ourselves and telling ourselves that all is lost. Usually people who tell themselves that all is lost soon begin to behave accordingly. Or, we can turn our circumstances into positive focus. A preacher once said, 'If you are entirely alone, so much the better: there is more room for God!'

This Advent many of us will feel that life has dealt us a terrible blow. Our plans have failed to work as we had hoped; we have never gained the profile or attention we feel our talents deserve; our personal progress plans are shattered and we have found that we're ill at ease with ourselves and the world.

Maybe Anna can teach us something. Perhaps it is a life of contemplation. But even if it's not, the space that has been created around us may give us options we didn't have before. How we use that space could well determine where we find ourselves when the moment of a lifetime comes our way. If we are busy with self-remorse we may not be tuned to it. If we are open to what God is doing in the world we may have opportunities to handle great possibilities.

Reflections on hope

- Was Anna hiding from her 'bad luck'? We can so easily mistake people who are devoted for people who opt out.
- Isn't it true that far too many people spend time hidden away behind closed doors under the guise of being devoted to God when in reality they are doing nothing more than escaping more important work which needs to be done?
- How do we focus on something positive if so much of our energy is taken up in the pain we feel about missed opportunities?
- Anna waited for a very long time before her big break. How long is too long and when should we move on to the next thing?

Creating space to act

Take some time to ask God how you should shape your life to make the best of your current situation.

Hope in Action

As the apostle James reminded us, faith without works is dead if it stands alone. Hope was never meant to be an idea without hands. The hope we have in Christ begins with our relationship with Him, but it will always rush in to serve those who are in need.

In our final study we take snapshots of the three events in the book of Acts which demonstrate faith at work, and remind ourselves that acts of kindness have always been expressions of hope in action.

29 DEC

Teaching and touching

Bible text
Acts 1:1

> In my former book, Theophilus, I wrote about all that Jesus
> began to do and to teach until the day he was taken up to
> heaven ...

I think this is one of the most sublime openings of any of the books
in the Bible.

Having completed his Gospel, Luke the doctor-come-historian
seems anxious to complete the sequel. Perhaps Theophilus was
anxious to read it. And this book, which will plot the amazing
success of the Christian Church in its infancy and early development,
goes straight to the heart of the matter.

Jesus taught and touched people.

It is impossible to read the Bible and miss the fact that faith
involves touching people where they hurt. Hope needs action.
This was Jesus' unmistakable teaching in Matthew's Gospel (Matt.
25:31–46). Faith has always been wedded to action. And with Jesus,
invariably this action was the restoration of wholeness to people in
need of practical help. Jesus fed huge crowds, touched lepers and
restored the lame and invalid. Many of His miracles were calculated
to make people socially adjusted. If a leper was healed he was
restored to his family and friends. If a cripple was made well he
became an economically viable person.

The early Christians were quite clear that Jesus didn't just preach;
He went about doing good things and healing the oppressed

(Acts 10:38). Now, here in the book of Acts, this will be an integral part of the mission of the Church in the world. This was to be a community which shared and cared (Acts 4:32–34).

All of us have been called to do good works. This is in fact why we have experienced God's grace. From the very beginning of time it was a part of our calling as people of hope (Eph. 2:8–10).

Doing hope

Good deeds really matter, and touching people can be quite simple.

When I was a pastor in East London, Barbara became a member of our local church and told us what had attracted her to the congregation: shortly after her father died I had visited her home.

. It wasn't anything I said. It was much more basic than that. As I approached the house, she and her siblings were sitting on the steps leading up to the door. Their mother – a faithful member of the congregation – tried to shoo them out of my way but I insisted it was OK and joined them on the steps. They couldn't believe it. She came to church and came to faith because the pastor sat with them on the stairs to their front door.

We can bring hope in a thousand simple ways, and most of us have opportunities to 'sit on the steps' with the people we meet on a daily basis. However simple it might seem, it really can go a very long way. There is something very powerful about just being there with people who need to be touched by the hope we have.

Reflections on hope

- The problem is that so often people focus on the really difficult things we can do to bring hope. However, not long ago my local pastor was preaching about opening the green gate outside his children's school for others to walk through. He does this for fifteen seconds every Monday to Thursday morning. He has become the green gate man! He's very proud of it.
- Are there opportunities being missed in your local fellowship to touch people nearby?

Creating space to act

Father God, in this season of goodwill, help me to be a person of hope to those in my community. Amen.

30 DEC

Hope is kindness

Bible text

Acts 4:8–10

> Then Peter, filled with the Holy Spirit, said to them: 'Rulers and elders of the people! If we are being called to account today for an act of kindness shown to a cripple and are asked how he was healed, then know this, you and all the people of Israel: It is by the name of Jesus Christ of Nazareth ... that this man stands before you healed.'

If I were involved in a high profile healing I wouldn't naturally think of it as 'an act of kindness', but that is precisely how Peter described the incredible miracle of this man's healing.

Peter was being very bold with it too. He was more than aware of the challenge before him. He was, after all, speaking to the Jewish high council, who exercised power over life and death. As far as they were concerned this healing that took place in the name of Jesus was an act of defiance. It was disturbing the status quo and threatening their very authority. But Peter called it 'kindness'.

And he was right to do so, for kindness speaks of God's generosity and care for people who need hope. In effect this first miracle, following the experience at Pentecost, was the insignia of the Jesus people. Along with the powerful preaching of the apostles it was to be these acts of kindness that would distinguish them as people who had been commissioned by Christ.

Kindness is more than social work or activism. It is not the product of our pain but God's response to our wellbeing. It comes from the very heart of God's strong compassion for people of all kinds in all kinds of situation. Kindness produces the sort of behaviour that brings hope and help to those who are in deep distress.

Doing hope

In this story Peter and the disciples put themselves at risk in order to bring hope to a man who was desperately in need of help. In later years this was to become a very typical response of the 'Parabolani'. *Parabolani* was a special team of Christians who served the community – sometimes at the cost of their own lives. In fact 'parabolani' means 'to expose oneself'. In public gatherings they were illegal, but they did take part in public life.

In the aftermath of Hurricane Katrina in 2005 the socialist politician and columnist Roy Hattersley wrote an evaluation of the Salvation Army's involvement in the tragedy. An atheist himself, Hattersley's article in the *Guardian* newspaper concluded that although he couldn't accept the Bible, 'men and women who, like me, cannot accept the mysteries and miracles do not go out with the Salvation Army at night ... The truth may make us free. But it has not made us as admirable as the average captain in the Salvation Army.'[1]

In today's Britain over 43 per cent of churches are involved in regular acts of hope; and they do this without asking for anything in return. These great good news stories often go unheralded in our news items, but in quiet and persistent ways the followers of Christ continue to offer hope through acts of kindness.

Reflections on hope

- Many of us would be somewhat cautious about offering hope in situations where we might be at risk. How do we get that balance right?
- How do we capture God's kindness, not just as activity, but as a key quality for our lives?
- How might our local congregations become much more like modern *parabolani* centres, sending out people for other people's benefit?

Creating space to act

Does our contribution count if it costs us nothing?

---

1. Roy Hattersley, 'Faith does breed charity' in the *Guardian* newspaper, 12 September 2005.

31 DEC

Restoring hope

Bible text
Acts 9:36

> In Joppa there was a disciple named Tabitha (which, when translated, is Dorcas), who was always doing good and helping the poor.

You could easily overlook this touching story of Dorcas. She was a minor figure who played such a major role in her neighbourhood that the Christians in Joppa sent word to Peter, who was in a nearby town called Lydda, to come and pray for her (Acts 9:37–38). It's more than likely that she was sick when they first sent for Peter, but by the time he reached Joppa, Dorcas was dead. In one of the most dramatic miracles in the New Testament Peter revived her, and with her the hope of the community she had served.

Her service was not spectacular. It seems Dorcas was a seamstress (v.39) and had poured this particular talent into the neighbourhood. There is no hint as to whether she sold her items, produced them cheaply or gave them away to the poor, but her acts of hope made her an indispensable addition to the community. Who would have thought that a woman's good deeds would have so endeared her to this community that they insisted on redirecting a senior apostle, begging him to restore her to them.

The outcome was even more amazing: many people came to faith in Christ as a result of this (v.42).

Doing hope

The Christian faith has produced many Dorcases over the years. On the walls of Pip 'n Jay (St Philip and St Jacob's Church), Christ Church, Bristol, there is a plaque which says,

> Mrs Ann Baskerfield of Leighton in the County of Bedford who died in Bristol 1st May 1802 aged 50 years.
> Her Chief Delight was in Doing Good.

As we come to the close of our Advent reflections and anticipate a new year, this is a great moment to be on the look-out for new opportunities of hope in which we can participate.

As I write this I look forward to Hope08. Millions of hours of kindness and good news will be shared across the UK for an entire year – and beyond – as hundreds of thousands of men and women perform acts of kindness in the name of Christ! The year 2008 promises to be a time in which the message of hope and God's love will be heard and experienced in towns, villages and cities across the UK.

The hope that Advent brings should live with us throughout the months and years ahead, and we should take every opportunity that comes our way to be agents of hope. When we do we will make a difference to the lives of others and, like Dorcas, we may find that they too come to believe in the Christ of Advent.

Reflections on hope

- Perhaps we might make a special effort to look out for some of the key opportunities to bring hope in the coming year. There are a host of organisations and events you can plug into.
- As we prepare to enter the New Year, with all the things planned for the next twelve months and beyond, it would be really helpful to pray for those who provide leadership in some of the things we have heard about.
- There will be many opportunities to get involved in short-term events in the coming months, but it would also be good to consider involvement with something for the long haul. What might that be?

Creating space to act

And we rejoice in the hope of the glory of God. Not only so, but we also rejoice in our sufferings, because we know that suffering produces perseverance; perseverance, character; and character, hope. And hope does not disappoint us, because God has poured out his love into our hearts by the Holy Spirit, whom he has given us.
(Rom. 5:2–5)

National Distributors

UK: (and countries not listed below)
CWR, Waverley Abbey House, Waverley Lane, Farnham, Surrey GU9 8EP.
Tel: (01252) 784700 Outside UK (44) 1252 784700

AUSTRALIA: CMC Australasia, PO Box 519, Belmont, Victoria 3216.
Tel: (03) 5241 3288 Fax: (03) 5241 3290

CANADA: Cook Communications Ministries, PO Box 98, 55 Woodslee Avenue, Paris, Ontario N3L 3E5.
Tel: 1800 263 2664

GHANA: Challenge Enterprises of Ghana, PO Box 5723, Accra.
Tel: (021) 222437/223249 Fax: (021) 226227

HONG KONG: Cross Communications Ltd, 1/F, 562A Nathan Road, Kowloon.
Tel: 2780 1188 Fax: 2770 6229

INDIA: Crystal Communications, 10-3-18/4/1, East Marredpalli, Secunderabad – 500026, Andhra Pradesh.
Tel/Fax: (040) 27737145

KENYA: Keswick Books and Gifts Ltd, PO Box 10242, Nairobi.
Tel: (02) 331692/226047 Fax: (02) 728557

MALAYSIA: Salvation Book Centre (M) Sdn Bhd, 23 Jalan SS 2/64, 47300 Petaling Jaya, Selangor.
Tel: (03) 78766411/78766797 Fax: (03) 78757066/78756360

NEW ZEALAND: CMC Australasia, PO Box 303298, North Harbour, Auckland 0751.
Tel: 0800 449 408 Fax: 0800 449 049

NIGERIA: FBFM, Helen Baugh House, 96 St Finbarr's College Road, Akoka, Lagos.
Tel: (01) 7747429/4700218/825775/827264

PHILIPPINES: OMF Literature Inc, 776 Boni Avenue, Mandaluyong City.
Tel: (02) 531 2183 Fax: (02) 531 1960

SINGAPORE: Alby Commercial Enterprises Pte Ltd, 95 Kallang Avenue #04-00, AIS Industrial Building, 339420.
Tel: (65) 629 27238 Fax: (65) 629 27235

SOUTH AFRICA: Struik Christian Books, 80 MacKenzie Street, PO Box 1144, Cape Town 8000.
Tel: (021) 462 4360 Fax: (021) 461 3612

SRI LANKA: Christombu Publications (Pvt) Ltd, Bartleet House, 65 Braybrooke Place, Colombo 2.
Tel: (9411) 2421073/2447665

TANZANIA: CLC Christian Book Centre, PO Box 1384, Mkwepu Street, Dar es Salaam.
Tel/Fax: (022) 2119439

USA: Cook Communications Ministries, PO Box 98, 55 Woodslee Avenue, Paris, Ontario N3L 3E5, Canada.
Tel: 1800 263 2664

ZIMBABWE: Word of Life Books (Pvt) Ltd, Christian Media Centre, 8 Aberdeen Road, Avondale, PO Box A480
Avondale, Harare.
Tel: (04) 333355 or 091301188

For email addresses, visit the CWR website: www.cwr.org.uk

CWR is a registered charity - Number 294387

CWR is a limited company registered in England - Registration Number 1990308

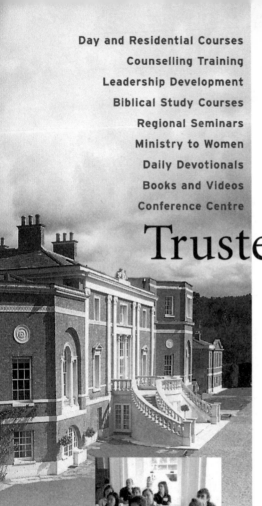

Day and Residential Courses
Counselling Training
Leadership Development
Biblical Study Courses
Regional Seminars
Ministry to Women
Daily Devotionals
Books and Videos
Conference Centre

Trusted all Over the World

CWR HAS GAINED A WORLDWIDE reputation as a centre of excellence for Bible-based training and resources. From our headquarters at Waverley Abbey House, Farnham, England, we have been serving God's people for 40 years with a vision to help apply God's Word to everyday life and relationships. The daily devotional *Every Day with Jesus* is read by nearly a million readers an issue in more than 150 countries, and our unique courses in biblical studies and pastoral care are respected all over the world. Waverley Abbey House provides a conference centre in a tranquil setting.

For free brochures on our seminars and courses, conference facilities, or a catalogue of CWR resources, please contact us at the following address.

CWR, Waverley Abbey House, Waverley Lane, Farnham, Surrey GU9 8EP, UK

Telephone: +44 (0)1252 784700
Email: mail@cwr.org.uk
Website: www.cwr.org.uk

 Applying God's Word
to everyday life and relationships

Other Advent books from CWR

Immanuel – God with Us

Are you looking for help in bringing spiritual
focus to Christmas? If so, this 31-day
inspirational guide through Advent, written
by respected author Anne Le Tissier, will
energise and inspire. Suitable for individual
or group study.

ISBN: 978-1-85345-390-8
£6.99 (plus p&p)

Advent Joy

These daily devotions for December seek to
recapture the true joy of Jesus's birth through
the study of biblical characters, hymns,
prayers, Christian testimony and personal
observations. Each day has a Bible reading,
meditation and points for discussion.

ISBN: 978-1-85345-356-4
£6.99 (plus p&p)

A Journey Through Advent

A thought-provoking book to help you make
your own journey with some of the key
characters of the Advent season. As you walk
alongside them, you will be strengthened
for your personal journey. For individual or
group use.

ISBN: 978-1-85345-312-0
£5.99 (plus p&p)

Prices correct at time of printing

Cover to Cover Complete

Now incorporating the full Bible text, this takes you on a chronological
journey through the Bible, allowing you to follow the events as they
happened – and to see more clearly the unfolding of God's purpose over
the centuries. It is structured to encourage you to read the entire Bible
text in one year, and with maps, charts, illustrations, diagrams, timelines
and notes, it will bring the Bible alive as never before.

ISBN: 978-1-85345-433-2
Introductory offer: £17.99 (plus p&p)
until 31 December 2007!
Normal RRP £19.99 (plus p&p)

Available: mid-September

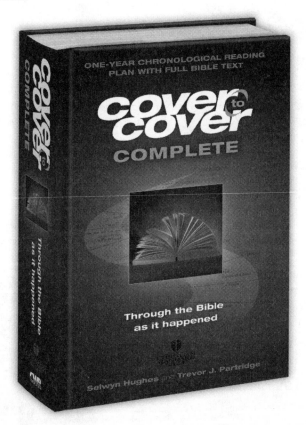